MIZORAM
AND
LOOK EAST POLICY

MIZORAM AND LOOK EAST POLICY

Lal Thanzaua Pudaite

AKANSHA PUBLISHING HOUSE
NEW DELHI • GUWAHATI • VISAKHAPATNAM

AKANSHA PUBLISHING HOUSE
4649-B/21, Ansari Road
Daryaganj, New Delhi-110002
Phones: 23268193, 09435116718
Email: ektabooks@yahoo.com
visit us: www.akanshapublishinghouse.com

Mizoram and Look East Policy

First Published 2010

ISBN 978-81-8370-221-8

PRINTED IN INDIA

Published by Akansha Publishing House, New Delhi-110002 and printed at S.N. Offset Press, Delhi.

In loving Memory of
my dear Husband
Mr. ***Lal Thanzaua Pudaite***

Contents

Foreword

My husband Lal Thanzaua Pudaite and I were married for 37 years and spent almost 30 years abroad because of his job. He became my best friend, my guide and anchor, my dependable supporter in everything. My whole world turned upside down when he passed away on the 25th of September 2008 at the age of 71 years. I was devastated and deeply distressed. I felt drained and empty, almost like a skeleton aimlessly moving around. I thought I should share the precious memories of my husband, a glimpse of the person he was. May be some will empathize with my great loss.

He was born in a small village of Khawlek in 1938. His mother died, after a long illness when he was only 12 years old. Being the eldest of four children, he could barely attend school. He just managed to pass his Matriculation while tending his paddy field. In 1958 he enrolled in Union Christian College, Barapani, Meghalaya; and studied Philosophy (Hons). He joined the Indian Foreign Service in 1966.

At the time of our marriage, I had no idea, nor could I imagine what the future would be like. He always reassured me "Together we will face the world." Just as unlike as we were in nature and personality, so also was our upbringing. I grew up in Aizawl (the capital of Mizoram) the youngest of eight children of a businessman. Our mother died when I was only eight years old and being the youngest meant an abundance of attention from everyone around, hardly any responsibilities and doing very much what I pleased without much thought for others.

Sometimes it's hard for two very different personalities to live together and be together. The road could be difficult and bumpy. But being a man of understanding and great depth, he never harbored any ill will towards anybody even though he could be very angry. Knowing I still had to learn a lot about life, he skillfully and patiently guided and encouraged me at all times. He was an upright man and upheld his principles and values. "Truth prevails" was his motto in life and held himself accountable for his actions. He would often say "My life is an open book" and "Let my children know me as I am."

His collection of essays "Dawn Tisei" is thought provoking, insightful and philosophical—just the kind of person he was. He liked learning new languages and learned them easily. Never one to do things in half measure he usually mastered any language that he undertook to learn. In Hongkong, when he studied Chinese language, he broke the University record that nobody had been able to break in 40 years.

Some may say I am overly praising him. There may be some truth to that. He definitely had his faults and weaknesses and those often proved to be the bumps and rough patches in our married life. But his basic goodness and humanness always won me over every time. Several years into our marriage I could quite easily say "his views are my views."

We live in Aizawl since he retired from service in 2000. Our children are grown up and live abroad. All the years during my husband's service, part of our duty was to meet new people and interact with them whether we liked it or not. After all this we looked forward to spending our time the way we wanted to, doing what we wanted. The two of us were quite content to be on our own. He subscribed many national and international magazines and he called them 'our windows to the world'. We enjoyed living in our own house and innocently supposed that we would spend many more years together. When friends told us "You two will live a long life; you exercise regularly, you eat healthy and your house and garden are ideal." We readily agreed with them. We really did think we were healthy. In fact, from the time we got married, my husband had never been seriously ill to actually need being nursed. Unfortunately what we didn't know was that he was suffering from a very serious but silent heart disease which did not manifest itself until it was too late. He died just two months after he was diagnosed with the heart problem." If only he hadn't been that strong and silent. If only he had complained sometimes. He must have had some days when he wasn't feeling good" is my pitiable lament now.

My husband never forgot his origins. This made him duty bound to help those in need. I would tell him, "If you take it on yourself to help all the needy, it's quite troublesome and difficult for me, we have more than enough burden within our families." He never forgot those who had helped during his childhood years and during his college days. He repaid them many times over. He maintained a bank account for his father which would transfer money to his father's account automatically each month and which he called "my Father's pension." He was determined to make his father's life as comfortable as possible.

When our children were young, his work kept us very busy many nights. I therefore suggested putting them in a boarding school because we don't seem to have enough time for them. My husband flatly refused. He said, "Nobody else loves them more than we do so why should we put them in somebody else's care." Although he didn't spend too much time with them, he was a good listener and gave much importance to their opinions and to what they told him.

Our son who has been away from home from the age of 16 years, told visitors at the time of his father's death : My father never troubled himself over material things, wealth or fame, he would tell us "a ho mai mai" meaning - it's not important/ no big deal. In spite of his busy works, he always put his duty as father, son, husband and brother above everything else. Because of his dedication and sacrifice as a father I can say I am what I am today. He often told us "We are happy when you are happy....." I have realized how wrong I was when I used to say to him. "You take your work too seriously and when you are home you are always reading. This way your children won't know you."

When I look back at my husband's life, it is not difficult for me to say that he made a success of his life. He had an outstanding service record and reached the pinnacle of his career as far as his service years allowed. After retirement he was re-employed for 3 years by the Government of India to look after Trade and Commerce in Taiwan. When we finally came home to Mizoram in 2000, he announced that he could dedicate his time now to help the poor and the needy. His efforts and works did not go unnoticed and so the Government of Mizoram offered him the post of Consultant in the Agriculture Department. He gladly accepted the post but refused any salary or other benefits as a rank of Minister of State. As was usual of my husband, he gave a hundred percent of himself to his work. Friends would joke and say "Your husband does not know how to retire."

I know I am more fortunate in many ways than many who had experienced what I had gone through. But this doesn't lessen how much I miss my husband or the dread that engulfs me when I think of living and facing the future without him. " All the World is Lonely Now."

– Lani Pudaite

1

MIZORAM*

1. Physical Features

Location

Mizoram lies in the north east end of India, much of its southern part sandwiched between Bangladesh and Myanmar. It is situated between 21.56 to 24.31 degrees north latitude and 92.16 to 93.26 degrees east longitude, extending over a land area of 21,087 square kilometers. The Tropic of Cancer passes by the capital city, Aizawl. The length of the state from north to south is 277 km. At the broadest from east to west, it is 121 km.

Its major length in the west borders the Chittagong Hill Tracts of Bangladesh, spanning 318 km. In the east and the south, its border with the Chin Hills and Northern Arakans of Myanmar extends to about 404 km. On the Indian side, Mizoram is bounded by the states of Assam, Manipur and Tripura. The length of its borders with these states extends over 123 km, 95 km. and 66 km, respectively.

Districts-8; Sub-Divisions-15; Development Blocks-22; Villages-817; Towns-22; City-1. There are no City or Town Councils. These are administered by Local administration Department (LAD) of the State Government. Autonomous District Councils - 3, namely, the Chakma, Lai and Mara District Councils in the southern region.

---

* Written for Institute of Developing Economies, Japan External Trade Organization (JETRO) and Published in 2005.

Geography & Natural Resources

The mountain ranges in Mizoram run from north to south and largely taper from the middle of the state towards the north, the west and the south. The ranges in the west are steep and precipitous while those in the east are somewhat gentler. The average height of the hills in the west is 1000 meters, gradually rising to 1,300 meters in the east. There are several mountain peaks of medium height. The highest peak in Mizoram is Phawngpui (Blue Mountain), which is 2,157 m. high and is located in the southeastern part of the State.

Mizoram is interspersed with numerous rivers, streams and brooks. The important rivers in the northern part of the state, flowing northwards, are the Barak (Tuiruang) and its tributaries, the Tlawng (Dhaleshwari), the Tuirial (Sonai) and the Tuivai. The Tuivawl, a tributary of the Tuivai, is another important river in the area. The Barak, the Daleshwari, the Tuivai and the Sonai are navigable for considerable stretches. The Daleshwari in particular had been the main entry and exit routes for Mizoram through the ages. Forest produce like timber and bamboo are floated down the river from the interior of the hills to the plains of Cachar in Assam while food, consumer goods and merchandise are brought by boats from the Assam plains to the hills of Mizoram. Before fair weather road from Silchar in Cachar district of Assam to Aizawl was constructed during World War II, the administration depended entirely on this river for transportation of men and material. The Barak and the Tuivai constitute the borderline between Manipur and Mizoram and the two territories have through the centuries shared the facilities provided by these rivers.

The most important river in the southern region of the state is the Chhimtuipui (Kolodyne) with its four main tributaries—the Mat, the Tuichang, the Tiau and the Tuipui. The Kolodyne flows into Mizoram from Myanmar and turns west first and then southward within Mizoram and reenters Myanmar. Though interrupted by rapids, some stretches of the river in Mizoram are navigable. The Khawthlangtuipui (Karnaphuli) and its tributaries - the Tuichawng, the Phaireng, the Kau, the Deh and the Tuilianpui - form the western drainage system. The Karnaphuli enters Bangladesh at Demagiri; at its mouth sits the port city of Chittagong.

Much of the potential of the river systems and water resources in Mizoram remains largely unexploited. The utilization of the hydro-potential for generation of energy, for example, in whatever form, large scale, mini or micro, is still fractional. There has been a modest improvement in the supply of drinking water but the sector lacks rational and systematic approach. The current condition of water transportation is less than retrogressive, partly because of the non-availability of transit facilities through Bangladesh.

There are three small plains in the state scattered over the mainly hilly terrain. The plains have thick layers of rich alluvial soil. The largest of these plains is the Champhai Plains, 10 km long and 5 km wide, and is situated near the Myanmar border, 150 km to the east of Aizawl. Another plain area is at Vanlaiphai, 90 km away to the southeast of Aizawl. It is 10 km long and ¾ km wide on average. The third such area is at Thenzawl, 100 km south of Aizawl. These plains have been put mainly to paddy cultivation. In addition, there are several small level grounds beside some of the rivers, which have been developed for wet rice cultivation.

The common rocks found in Mizoram are sandstone, shale, silt stone, clay stone and slates. The rock system is weak and unstable, prone to seismic influence. Soils vary from sandy loam and clayey loam to clay, generally mature but leached owing to steep gradient and heavy rainfall. The "soils are porous with poor water holding capacity, deficient in potash, phosphorous, nitrogen and even humus. The pH shows acidic to neutral reaction due to excessive leaching." (Environment & Forest Department Report, 2003).

According to the report (2003) of the Department of Environment and Forests, 83 per cent of the total area of the state (21,087 sq. km.) is covered by forests. However, due to the traditional practice of shifting cultivation called *'jhuming'*, uncontrolled fire, unregulated felling and arbitrary allotment of land to individuals, two-third of the area is reported to have been partly depleted and degraded. [Update, 2007-2008: Reserved Forest : 6465 sq. km, Protected Forest 941 sq. km].

The different types of land cover in Mizoram as estimated by Landsat Imagery are shown below: (sources: Department of Environment and Forest)

Different Types of Land Cover in Mizoram

	Type of Land Cover	*Area (in sq.km)*
1.	Closed (good) forest	4,190
2.	Closed forest affected by shifting cultivation	13,520
3.	Forest degraded by shifting cultivation	2,600
4.	Non-forest	640
5.	Water bodies	140
	Total	21,090

Bamboo

Mizoram has abundant natural bamboo resources. Around 57 per cent of the area of the state is covered by bamboo forests, located in the areas ranging in height from 400 m to 1500 m above the mean sea level. These forests are situated mainly in the river banks and abandoned jhum lands, forming a dominant secondary vegetation.

Both the clump forming and non-clump forming bamboos are found in most parts of Mizoram. The exception is the high land parts of the eastern region. There are 20 species of bamboo in the state, of which *Melocanna baccifera*, locally called 'Mautak', is the dominant. Forming no clumps, it is a fast spreading bamboo. The culms grow up to 8-10 m tall and are extensively used for construction of houses in the rural areas, especially for walling and flooring, and temporary dwelling of various sorts. They are also used for furniture, fencing, weaving and pulping, but are not yet processed for industrial use. During rainy season, the shoots form an important item of food for the population. At present, the State Government claims to have received annually Rs. 8 million in revenue mainly from bulk sales of unprocessed bamboos. This is done through the *Mahal* system, a practice of contracting out the rights of harvesting bamboos to individuals or firms on payment of nominal royalties.

The dominant bamboo in northeast India, the *Melocanna baccifera* is said to have a life cycle of 48 years, at the end of which it flowers and bears fruits and dies. The fruits when eaten by rodents apparently increase the fertility of the latter, resulting in an explosion of the rat population in a short time. Once the bamboo fruits are exhausted, the rats turn to eating whatever foodgrains available in the farms or in storage, causing severe depletion of food supplies for the population and resulting in famine. Such occurrence on two occasions in the past has been recorded in Mizoram. The next flowering of the bamboos is forecast to occur in 2007.

Climate

Mizoram as a whole receives an average rainfall of about 3000 mm a year, with Aizawl getting 2380 mm and 3,178 mm for Lunglei in the south. Rainfall is usually evenly distributed throughout the state. During rains the climate in the lower hills and river gorges is highly humid and exhausting for people, whereas it is cool and pleasant in the higher hills even during the hot season. A rather peculiar characteristic of the climate is the incidence of violent storms during March-early May. Strong storms arise from the north-west and sweep over the entire hills, often causing extensive damages to 'kacha' (temporary) dwellings and flowering perennials.

Temperature varies from about 12 degrees C in winter

to 30 degrees C plus in summer. Winter is from November to February, with little or no rain during this period. Spring lasts from end February to mid-April. Heavy rains start in June and continue up to August. September and October are the autumn months when the rain is intermittent.

2. Socio-Political Structure

Historical Background

Except for those written after the advent of the British in the late 18th century, there is no recorded history of the Mizos. Some of the tribes living outside of Mizoram prefer to call themselves 'Zomis or simply Zos'; '*mi*' affixed to these terms means 'people or person/s'. The British variously referred to them as Lushais, Kukis (old or new Kukis, depending on the period of their contacts with the tribes) and Chins in Myanmar. All modern historians belonging to the various tribes, however, agree that all the tribal groups inhabiting the immediate neighborhood of the present state of Mizoram - in such areas as in Myanmar, Bangladesh, Tripura, Assam and Manipur - once belonged to the same proto-tribe. They often refer to themselves collectively as 'Zo Hnahthlak', people of Zo ancestry, origin or progeny.

While some of the tribes living outside Mizoram such as the Hmars, the Paites, the Thadous or Kukis, etc. still prefer to assert their sub-group identities for practical political or other reasons, the trend toward integration in a larger identity is gradually gaining strength. This growing awareness of belonging to a larger identity has the potential to upset in future the balance of the existing political demarcations in the sub-region.

Despite the absence of recorded history, most researchers conclude that the Mizos came to their present abode from southern China, possibly Yunnan province, by gradual migration through northern Myanmar. Dietary practices, customs, traditional values, legends, oral history, folklore and linguistic affinity are some of the bases on which these investigations are conducted. Although there can be no certainty about the period in which the Mizos migrated to the present Chin Hills in Myanmar, it is generally believed that this took place about four to five hundred years ago. However, the Mizos of Mizoram appear to have arrived at their present settlement relatively recently, perhaps in the late 17th or early 18th century. Animesh Ray, a researcher of considerable thoroughness, put it in the early 18th century. (*Mizoram, India –The Land and The People* Series, 1993). As their oral history attests, the last wave of the migration of the Mizo tribes from Myanmar to India took place at about the time, or soon after, the institution of hereditary chieftainship gradually overtook their earlier practice of warrior chieftainship. Once hereditary rulers were installed, genealogy, even if orally passed on, became a reliable record of sort. Based on the genealogy of the chiefs, "early 18th century" appears to be the most likely period.

Traditional Institution

Although other Mizo tribes adopted and practiced hereditary chieftainship, the Sailo Chiefs of the Lusei or Lushai tribe were the most durable, perhaps, because they were the most enlightened. At any rate, their mode of governance became the norm for rural administration in much of the Mizo or Zo inhabited areas in pre-Independent northeast India. The British did little to interfere with the system of administration practiced by the Chiefs, except in rare cases of extraordinary misrule. Instead, they devised ways to ensure maintenance of law and order and social order through the Chiefs. Indeed, this practice of "indirect administration" was formally provided for in the Government of India Act, 1935, and on the basis of this Act, an official order, named 'Excluded and Partially Excluded Areas Order,' defining the areas to be covered, was issued by the King in Council on March 3, 1936.

The following paraphrase of an order issued by the Superintendent of Lushai Hills in 1898 also makes this clear:

1. Every Chief is responsible for all that goes on in his village. All orders affecting a village shall be sent to the Chief through the Circle Inspector (an official appointed by the British to liaise with the Chiefs).
2. Every Chief shall adjudicate all civil disputes between people of his village. He shall also dispose of all criminal cases, except those in which a person is killed or badly wounded. A Chief's order would not be interfered with unless he had acted in bad faith.
3. The Chiefs are responsible for ensuring that records are kept of the following:
   - i) All births and deaths in the village;
   - ii) All movements of people into or out of the village; and
   - iii) All changes in the licensed guns.

The authority of the Chief, though nearly absolute within his domain which may consist of one or more or a group of villages, was often restrained in practice by the Council of Elders (Upas), an advisory body appointed by the Chief to assist him in the performance of his duties. The members of this Council were usually so selected by the Chief as to represent and safeguard the interests of the different clans or sub-tribe groups among his subjects. Captain T.H. Lewin, a former British Administrator in Lushai Hills, was so impressed by the administrative system of the Mizo Chiefs that he described it as "a democracy tempered by despotism" worthy of being "classed among the visions of Utopian philosophy." (*Exercises in The Lushai Dialect*, 1874, London).

In return for his services, the Chief was entitled to: 1) Fathang - six bushels of rice grain from every household; 2) Sachhiah (Meat Tax) - anyone who bagged a four-legged big game must present him one of the hind legs; and 3) whenever his house required to be repaired or rebuilt, his subjects would do it for free.

Institution of Zawlbuk (Bachelor's Quarters)

Apart from the dispensation of the Chief and his Elders, the main instrument for ensuring discipline, instilling moral education, maintenance of law and order and the smooth functioning of the society was the institution of Zawlbuk. The exact date when this institution came about cannot be pinpointed. It is, however, certain that this tradition came to be established after the Mizos entered India and the Chief felt secure enough to regulate the management of social order for his subjects.

Though everyone was responsible to make sure that theft and other crimes were not committed, there had to be an organizing agency that was capable of ensuring this. This is what the Zawlbuk did. All boys from the age of about 10 to till they were married and had one or two children were required to sleep at Zawlbuk, a large dormitory like structure usually located in the middle of the village. This is where the boys were trained to fit themselves into society. Before a boy attained puberty, he was taught to shoulder his responsibilities for the community such as fetching water, collecting wood for use at the Zawlbuk, cleaning the Zawlbuk and its surrounding, and tending the Zawlbuk fire, which was used for lighting as well as for warmth. All the traditional values that the community held dear were passed on to the youth via the Zawlbuk life by way of practical demonstration.

A Historical Background

By the early thirties, Christianity, which entered Mizoram for the first time on January 11, 1894 via the Welsh Missionaries, had become the religion of the overwhelming majority of the Mizos. The Church had set up schools and rudimentary health services. Literacy was spreading fast. A few young Mizos had even gone to universities. At the same time, common people had begun to give up their old ways. Western ways of dressing and thinking had begun to spread, especially among the young men. Social life centered on the ways of Zawlbuk had gradually disappeared and had been replaced by that revolved around the Church. Through the organizing activities of the Church they begun to understand the advantages of forming groups for focused goals.

The mass movements of the times for Independence in mainstream India, too, inspired in a few young men as yet undefined ideas about possibilities in politics. And they started thinking in terms of organizing themselves for common purposes. Thus was born the first district-wide and secular organization, Young Mizo Association (originally named Young Lushai Association after the name of the District) on June 15, 1935. A missionary initially headed the association; and its objectives were entirely non-political, namely, 1) to use leisure for beneficial activities; 2) to serve for the welfare of the people; and 3) to promote Christian way of living. In the same year was founded the Mizo Zirlai Pawl (Mizo Students Union) with a motto: 'Unity is strength.' Its aim was to promote understanding, cooperation and unity among all Mizo students, regardless of whether they lived in Mizoram or outside. Both organizations grew rapidly and soon became effective vehicles for the promotion of fellow feeling and unity amongst the young Mizos of various regions.

World War II and the anticipation for Indian independence during the same period were really that set the Mizos to think about politics. Once Burma fell to the Japanese, Mizoram became the frontline. Near panicking British administrators mobilized the Chiefs and the people to pledge loyalty to the Imperial Crown and to resist the advance of the Japanese army at all costs. Even before the war, a large number of young Mizos had enlisted in the British Indian Army and many of them were now fighting alongside the British. And, naturally, the families and friends of these soldiers were inclined to side with the British.

At the same time, increasingly tense were the anxieties of the Mizos for their future in the new dispensation that was to follow independence of India. It is also obvious that the then British administrators of Mizoram had given them more than a hint that the Mizos could still have the option to opt out of the three dominions (India, Pakistan and Burma) to be created by the Independence of India Act, 1947 even as late as on August 14, 1947. Copies of the relevant documents are in Appendices. These documents as well as the Resolutions of the Chin-Lushai Conference held at Fort William, Calcutta in 1892 (also in the same appendix) were to form later the bases on which the Mizo National Front (MNF) 'declared' independence for Mizoram and resorted to insurgency in March, 1966.

Political Parties

Thus, the objectives of the first two political parties formed immediately preceding independence also reflected the anxieties and debates of the times.

The Mizo Union, formed on 9 April 1946, was first named Mizo Common People's Union, reflecting the anti-Chiefs sentiments of the common people. Many had suspected that the British, working with the Chiefs, were trying to encourage a policy of isolated independence for Lushai Hills or Mizoram. The District Conference that had been convened in January 1946 by the then Superintendent, A. R. H. McDonald to advise him on future administrative set up for the Hills had had half of its members composed of Chiefs, in the face of opposition by the commoners. To enlist the support of the elite and the enlightened and liberal chiefs, the name of the party was changed to Mizo Union. However, it remained a party of the common people.

As independence was drawing near, there were sharp differences of opinion regarding the future of Mizoram. Though the Mizo Union was in favour of staying within India, a secessionist group came up in the Party favouring merger with Burma. (Their long term goal though not specified appeared to be independence. The draft of the Burmese Constitution had included the right to secession by the States within ten years vide Chapter X). The group, supported by most of the Chiefs, broke away from Mizo Union and formed a party called the United Mizo Freedom Organisation (UMFO) on 5 July 1947.

In 25 January 1947 the Constituent Assembly of India (the drafting body of the Indian Constitution) appointed an Advisory Committee on minorities, tribal areas and related matters under the chairmanship of Sardar Vallabhbhai Patel. The Committee in turn constituted a Sub-Committee chaired by Gopinath Bardoloi for the northeastern tribal areas and the Excluded and Partially Excluded Areas. This became popularly known as the Bardoloi Sub-Committee and the members co-opted from Mizoram were Ch. Saprawnga and Khawtinkhuma, representatives of the Mizo Union.

On the basis of various memoranda submitted to it by political groups, including McDonald's District Conference and the Mizo Union, Bardoloi Sub-Committee in its Report to the Constituent Assembly suggested a special setup for the tribal areas. It recommended that the tribal people should be free from any fear of exploitation or domination by the advanced section of the people from the plains and that they should have full freedom with regard to their traditions, customs, inheritance, social organizations, village administration, etc. The pattern of administration recommended for the tribal areas in the northeast thus took shape in the Sixth Schedule to the Constitution.

Early Elected Bodies and Related Activities

After Independence, as a prelude to the District Council, a 35 member Advisory Council was created and the elections to the Council were held on 15 April 1948. The Mizo Union captured all the seats, except two won by the UMFO. The Mizo Union soon came into conflict with Superintendent L. L. Peters, who was openly siding with the Chiefs over the latter's role in future administration. The Mizo Union then launched non-cooperation movement in December 1948, which lasted till February 1949 and for months thereafter in some far-flung areas.

District Council: As envisaged by the Sixth Schedule to the Constitution of India, which was adopted on 26 January, 1952, six autonomous districts with District Councils came up in Assam - the Mizo District Council being one such district. Regional Council was set up in the Pawi-Lakher Region in southern Mizoram. The Advisory Council had been dissolved in November 1951 and the election to the District Council was held on 4 April 1952. The total strength of the Council was 24, of which 18 were to be elected and six nominated. Out of 18 seats, 17 were won by the Mizo Union and one by UMFO. The District Council was inaugurated by Bishnuram Medhi, Chief Minister of Assam on 25 April 1952.

Under the Constitution, the District Council has law making powers concerning:

(1) Management of land and forests other than reserve forest;

(2) Use of canal or water for the purpose of agriculture;

(3) Regulation of the practice of *jhum*;

(4) Establishment of village or town committee and matters relating to village or town administration including public health and sanitation.

(5) Appointment or succession of chiefs or headmen;

(6) Inheritance of property;

(7) Marriage and divorce; and

(8) Social customs.

The District Council also has the power to constitute village councils and courts, appoint its officers and to prescribe procedures.

The Regional Council exercises all these functions within its area. There are certain exclusive jurisdictions of the District Council, which covers primary schools and the medium of instruction for them, dispensaries, markets, cattle pounds, ferries, fisheries, roads and waterways. The District or Regional Council has financial powers to levy taxes, fees, tolls, etc. over the subjects it is empowered to legislate. It also has the power to control or regulate money lending or trading by non-tribals within its area.

The first budget of the Council in 1952-53 was RS. 17,175– which was mainly for establishment. From the start, the Council suffered from chronic financial inadequacy despite a grant announced by Prime Minister Jawharlal Nehru during his visit to Mizoram in October 1952.

Village Councils and the Abolition of Chieftainship: Through the sustained pressure of the Mizo Union, the Assam Government passed the Lushai Hills (Acquisition of the Chief's Rights) Act in 1954. In August 1954, the rights and interests of 259 Chiefs in the District Council area were taken over by the Council and the Regional Council assumed those of 50 Chiefs in the Pawi-Lakher Region. Village Councils were constituted to perform basically the same functions as hitherto discharged by the Chiefs and their *Upas*. The Mizo Union won the election to all the Village Councils, which was held on 24 July 1954, thus vindicating its stand for the abolition of chieftainship.

Demand for a Hill State: As they experienced some measure of autonomy within the confines of the Assam state, the Hills people started demanding for more. In 1953, the United Mizo Freedom Organisation (UMFO) passed a resolution demanding the formation of a hill state consisting of Manipur, Tripura, the Autonomous Districts of Assam and the North-eastern Frontier Agency (now Arunachal Pradesh). The attempt to impose the Assamese language as the official language of the state and the alleged discrimination by the Assam government against these areas were other reasons advanced. The resolution was one of several submitted to the States Reorganisation Commission (SRC), which was visiting Assam in 1954. (The Commission was charged to look into demands in various parts of India for re-demarcation of state boundaries or reconstitution of new states and to make recommendations to the Government of India). The Mizo Union also cited 'Assam's discrimination" against hill people as the source of the clamour for a separation from Assam and demanded for the integration of the Mizo inhabited areas of Manipur and Tripura with Mizo district.

The SRC did not recommend creation of a Hill State; instead urged a review of the powers and the functioning of the district councils. The Nagas had boycotted the SRC. Most tribal leaders and their people were unhappy with its recommendations. The leaders met at Aizawl in 1955 and formed the Eastern India Tribal Union (EITU) to demand the creation of a hill state comprising the hill districts of Assam. The UMFO merged with EITU. As some parties like the Mizo Union did not join the EITU, a more inclusive forum to work for the same demand was set up at a meeting of hill leaders at Shillong on 6 and 7 July 1960. The forum was called All Party Hill Leaders Conference (APHLC), which resolved at its meeting at Haflong in November 1960 that the hill districts should separate from Assam and form an eastern frontier state.

In 1961, Assamese became the official language of the state, amid vociferous protests by hill leaders. Disillusionment felt by the hill leaders with the government in Delhi and with the state authorities in Assam, in particular, crystallized into bitter opposition to their continued inclusion within Assam.

On its part, the Central Government offered what was termed the Scottish Pattern of autonomy, which still fell far short of the autonomy expected by the hill people, let alone, statehood. The Mizo Union boycotted outright the Commission designated to work out the details of the Pattern as it stuck to a demand for statehood for the Mizo populated areas. No Mizo leaders could afford to be moderate any longer. The more radical they appeared, the more they appeared to gain in popular support.

The Mizo National Front (MNF) and Insurgency

Such was the situation in Mizoram when Laldenga, the founder of the Mizo National Front, came on the political arena in 1961. Opportunely for him, a famine brought about by an explosion of rat population resulting from the flowering of bamboos (called *mautam*) had ravaged the entire Mizoram hills two years earlier. Resentment against the Assam government for its "delayed and negligent" famine relief operations was high. A number of voluntary bodies sprung up to provide relief to the famine stricken people. The Mizo National Famine Front launched by Laldenga in 1960 was one such an organization, which achieved a striking success in enlisting volunteers. The Front dropped the word "Famine" from its name and, on 22 October 1961, became the Mizo National Front (MNF), a political party with an avowed aim of achieving an independent and sovereign Mizoram. (A copy of the Memorandum submitted to the Prime Minister of India, demanding independence, is at Appendix VI). The party grew rapidly, especially amongst the youth. By 1963, it managed to gain in a bye-election two seats of the State Assembly vacated by the Mizo Union as well as 145 Village Councils. However, the Mizo Union retained its primacy in the rural areas, winning 220 Village Councils.

Insurgency: Once the MNF declared 'independence' as its goal, it followed that it would have to resort to armed struggle to try and force the Indian government to concede independence to Mizoram. After preparing for three years, on 28 February 1966, the MNF volunteers commenced an armed struggle for independence and attacked different Government stations all over Mizoram. On 1 March it declared independence for Mizoram. Laldenga and sixty others signed the declaration, which appealed to all independent countries to recognize 'independent' Mizoram. With some lulls in the fighting, the rebellion 'officially' lasted 20 years, till the MNF armed cadres laid down their arms upon the signing of the so-called Peace Accord in 1986, technically termed 'Memorandum of Settlement.' (See appendix).

A brief assessment of the insurgency movement as a whole, however, may be relevant. The primary question that has often been raised is whether Laldenga actually intended to lead the MNF into an open rebellion against the government of India. It has been argued that he was exploiting the disgruntled youth of the time in order to propel himself into political prominence. An ex-serviceman and ex-clerk of the District Council, suspended for misappropriation of funds, Laldenga had been a political nobody. He was no doubt an exceptionally charismatic demagogue. On the other hand, there was no doubt that most of the MNF cadres, particularly the educated and the armed cadres, had been fully aware of the inevitability of a protracted armed struggle and had been prepared for it, believing that independence would ultimately be a possibility. Even if Laldenga had not intended it originally, his own followers would have made rebellion inexorable. The question for him then really became how and when to end the insurgency.

According to Biakchhunga, who served as Chief of the MNF Army from 1971 to 1978 and then briefly acted as President, citing the urgency to "make contacts with foreign powers" Laldenga and his family along with a small escort left Mizoram for East Pakistan on the night of the uprising itself, i.e. 28 February 1966. He came back to Mizoram for about a week in December of that year to attend the first MNF Parliament Session at Sialsir village. These were the two occasions on which Laldenga was personally present in Mizoram throughout the duration of the rebellion. At the Parliament Sitting, Laldenga handed over the entire task of running the underground government that had been set up by the MNF to the Vice-President, Lalnunmawia, who kept his charge from December 1966 to May 1969. During this period, the bulk of the MNF underground activists remained within Mizoram. They then moved south to Chittagong Hills in East Pakistan in early 1969. On 20 May 1969, Laldenga again took over the Presidency of the MNF from Lalnunmawia. Since then, most of the rebel activities were carried out on specific missions directed from outside India. (Hnam Kalsiam or Nation Building, Biakchhunga, 1996 and personal interview with him).

Soon after Laldenga reclaimed the overall charge of the movement, he secretly sent Rozama and Vanlalngaia, ranking Intelligence Officers of the MNF, as emissaries to make contact with the officials of the Indian government. Though these messengers were arrested by the Indian Police at Karimganj on 5 July 1969, before they could reach Delhi, the result of their interrogations by the Police was bound to have been conveyed to the Indian Intelligence. It may thus be safely assumed that the Indian authorities became aware of Laldenga's readiness to end the insurrection on a bargain. Vanlalngaia said to this writer on 11 August 2004, "On that fateful day when Laldenga dispatched us to make peace overtures to the Indian officials, I realized that the struggle for independence ended then and there." This was around the time the 'sub-state' of Meghalaya, comprising the Garo Hills and the Khasi and Jaintia Hills, was being formed. Mikir hills and North Cachar Hills were given option to join the sub-state. It became apparent that Meghalaya, without firing a single bullet, would soon attain full statehood. The future of Mizo Hills, however, significantly remained to be decided.

As for Laldenga's "mission" to mobilize foreign governments for aid to the MNF movement, on account of which he had absented himself for nearly three years from the scene of the real struggle, his performance seemed rather dismal. The Inter Services Intelligence (ISI) of Pakistan, which was always looking for an opportunity to fish in India's troubled political waters, naturally facilitated his move to East Pakistan and later to West Pakistan or rather Pakistan after the creation of Bangladesh. Even the ISI did not seem to lavish him with funds. The current Chief Minister of Mizoram, Zoramthanga, then Private Secretary to Laldenga, often speaks today in public speeches of the times when they had to "pray" all night to God to provide them with needed funds and of how miraculously they were always provided. The reason behind the ambivalence of the ISI towards the MNF must have arisen from the suspicion that Laldenga was not resolute in the struggle he had initiated, a suspicion that was beginning to exasperate the educated cadres of the MNF soon after the move to East Pakistan. China's assistance to MNF either in the form of weapons or training seemed nominal. It was also apparently a one time affair and, according to Biakchhunga, it was discontinued due to "difficulties of communication."

It became clear that from late 1969 onwards, Laldenga was secretly searching ways to make contact and commence negotiations with the government of India. However, this was about the time India was preoccupied with the liberation movement in East Pakistan and later with the birth pangs of Bangladesh. Apparently, the impending fall of East Pakistan greatly demoralized the MNF leadership. Zoramthanga, the then Private Secretary to Laldenga, even proposed on 16 December 1971 that they might surrender to the advancing Indian forces at Subalong (Biakchhunga).The main forces of the MNF were also later occupied in settling down in the Arakan Hills of Myanmar, as they could no longer stay in independent Bangladesh. As Laldenga and his personal staff were on their way to Islamabad, former Vice-President, Lalnunmawia and a Minister, R. Zamawia were deputed on 18 December 1971 once again to sound out the Indian authorities for peace talks.

It was only since November 1973, after Laldenga settled down in Pakistan, that regular contacts between the MNF and Indian authorities begun. In a letter to Prime Minister Indira Gandhi dated 20 August 1975, Laldenga stated, "Since November 1973, my officials have been meeting your representatives to discuss the question of restoration of peace and normalcy in Mizoram...." In this letter, he asserted that the solution of the Mizoram problem could be found within the framework of the Indian Constitution and revealed that his senior colleagues did not know as yet his overtures to the Indian government. He requested "the utmost secrecy" be kept about his peace moves and sought the help of the government in persuading his radical colleagues to come to the negotiating table.

The story after this in a nutshell was that of Laldenga and his coterie working together with the Indian Intelligence in the attempt to "persuade" the "radical elements" in the MNF to accept a settlement within the Indian Constitution. Those who could not be persuaded were pressured or sidelined or marginalized. However, it took much effort and time before the entire MNF outfit could be brought around to agree to cease fire. Settlement could perhaps have come earlier, but for the fact that the political situation within Mizoram from 1979 to 1984 was such that no arrangement could be made for Laldenga to become the Chief Minister without election, the minimum prize that he would have wished for, for giving up arms. During this period, the People's Conference Party, a regional political party, was in power and the Chief Minister, Brigadier (Rtd) Thenphunga Sailo would not give up his office unless he was defeated in an election.

It was only after the Indian National Congress (I), a party that could be directed and controlled from Delhi came to power in 1984 that the prospect for peace in Mizoram became bright. The then Chief Minister, Lal Thanhawla offered to vacate his office in favour of the MNF chief Laldenga if that would facilitate the peace negotiations, much to the relief of the people who were by now extremely frustrated at the protracted negotiations.

After resumption of talks in late 1984, the two sides finally came to a settlement in early 1986. The Memorandum of Settlement was signed on 30 June 1986. The text of the accord is in the Appendices.

As provided for in the agreement between the Indian National Congress and the MNF, upon the signing of the peace accord Laldenga was installed as the Chief Minister of Mizoram on 21 August 1986. Before the signing of the accord, Laldenga had amended the constitution of the MNF making it a political party. The MNF became a regional party in Mizoram.

Major Political Parties

Indian National Congress

The District Branch of the Indian National Congress was established by A. Thanglura on 11 April 1961 when Mizoram was still one of the districts of Assam. Its presence in Mizoram remained uneventful and lacking in influence till the election to the fourth and last District Council in April 1970, in which the Congress won 10 out of 18 elected seats. In the election to the newly created Union Territory of Mizoram held in April 1972, it won six seats whereas the Mizo Union got 21 seats out of the 27 elected members. Soon after this election, the Mizo Union, which had formed the government in the Union Territory, decided to merge with the Congress. Since then, the party has been playing a leading role in the affairs of Mizoram, either as the ruling government or in opposition.

For the first time the Congress came on its own into power in Mizoram in the 1984 election to the UT Assembly. It won 20 seats against 8 by the PC. Lal Thanhawla, the President of the party, became the youngest Chief Minister in the country on May 5, 1984. Upon the conclusion of the peace settlement between the MNF and the central government, however, Lal Thanhawla vacated the Chief Minister's office and the MNF President, Laldenga became the Chief Minister on August 21, 1986. He became the Deputy Chief Minister instead.

After a short break, the Congress again formed the Mizoram government, upon winning the sixth Assembly election in 1989 with 23 MLAs out of the 40 seats. The last time the Congress came into power was in the election to the Assembly held on November 3, 1993. It contested the election jointly with the Mizoram Janata Dal, a name briefly assumed by the People's Conference party led by Brig. T. Sailo. The two parties together won 24 seats as against 14 by the MNF and two Independents. Though the People's Conference Party or Janata Dal withdrew from the coalition government after 5 months, with the support of eight MLAs who defected from the MNF and the PC, the Congress government managed to serve its full term. In the State elections held after this, in 1998 and 2003, the Congress won only 6 and 12 seats respectively and thus had to be in opposition.

To some justification, the Congress has been blamed for bringing corruption into the politics of Mizoram. Its refusal to continue development plans initiated by its predecessor Ministry, the Sailo government, is responsible for the lack of infrastructure in Mizoram. And these are the main reasons for its failure to come back into power. Credit must be given to the introduction by the Congress of the New Land Use Policy (NLUP), a plan to replace the practice of jhuming by settled cultivation, even though it was largely unsuccessful. The concept behind the policy has highlighted the seriousness of the problem.

Lal Thanhawla remains the President of the Party and as the leader of the largest group of MLA's (12) in opposition, he is the official Leader of the Opposition in the State Assembly. At present, the party is the second largest political party in Mizoram. (Update: The Indian National Congress led by Lalthanhawla won the Assembly election in 2008 by absolute majority)

Mizo National Front (MNF).

Founded on 22 October 1961 as a revolutionary party to fight for independence of Mizoram by Laldenga, it was transformed into a normal political party on the day of the signing of the peace accord between it and the government of India. Upon the death of Laldenga, Zoramthanga was elected President of the party and remains so till today.

For the first time, the MNF contested the 1987 election and won with a 25 members majority. Congress won 13 and PC two. Its rule was, however, short-lived. As two of its MLAs broke away from the party on August 9, 1988, the Ministry was reduced to a minority and the Assembly had to be dissolved. After a brief President's Rule, another election was held on January 21, 1989, in which the Congress replaced the MNF government.

In the next two terms of the State Assembly, the MNF remained in opposition and staged a come back only in the 1998 election. It fought the election jointly with the MPC and the two parties together won 33 seats. Zoramthanga, the MNF leader, was installed as the Chief Minister while the MPC President, Lalhmingthanga, became the Deputy Chief Minister. As the MNF on its own has a majority in the legislature, the MPC members were evicted from the Ministry within less than a year. In the last Assembly election held on November 20, 2003, the MNF won 21 seats; and in alliance with two independents and 1 former MPC member, it formed the present Ministry. It thus remains the largest political party in Mizoram.

Corruption in high places appears to be less rampant in the present MNF government than it was in the time of the Congress. However, its practice of openly bestowing favours to loyal party workers is its drawback. While such a practice may earn votes at the time of elections, it prevents the government departments from fully focusing on development works. It has also yet to work out a thorough going plan for infrastructure development, for example, in the energy sector, without which no effective development proggrammes can be pursued in Mizoram.

Mizoram People's Conference (MPC)

Upon retirement from the Army in early 1974, Brigadier Thenphunga Sailo set up a Human Rights Committee to monitor and record human rights abuse and excesses committed by the security forces, especially on the innocent civilians, in the course of their operations against the insurgents. The reports prepared by this group were brought to the notice of the central government, with the result that the security forces became more careful and less high-handed in their operations. The Human Rights Committee became very popular and many people hailed Brigadier T. Sailo as a father figure and protector.

With a view to playing an effective role in the affairs of Mizoram, the Committee thought of setting up a political party and convened a general conference of people of all walks of life. The conference decided to form a political party named 'People's Conference' (PC) on April 17, 1975. Brig. T. Sailo was elected the first President. It was the first party in Mizoram, which clearly defined its objectives, particularly with regard to development plans for the territory. Its candidate, Dr. Rothuama won the 1976 Parliamentary election with an impressive margin.

In the second election to the Mizoram Assembly, PC won 23 out of 30 seats and its President Brig. T. Sailo became Chief Minister on June 2, 1978. However, due to internal dissension, the PC government fell; the Assembly was dissolved and President's Rule had to be imposed on November 11, 1978. After five months of President's Rule, fresh elections to the Assembly were held again. This time also, the People's Conference won a majority of 18 MLAs and new Ministry headed by Sailo was sworn in on May 8, 1979. The ministry served its full term of five years but was ousted in the 1984 election by the Congress (I). For the first time in Mizoram, the Sailo government embarked upon infrastructure development for energy, transport and communications, rail links, etc. Despite the continuing insurgency situation, it managed to lay substantial foundation for future development work. However, these development foundations have not been consistently pursued by successive ministries till today.

The PC party was later renamed 'Mizoram People's Conference (MPC) party. Apart from briefly sharing power in coalition ministries with the Congress(I) in 1994 and with the MNF in 1998, it has not been in power since 1989. With only two MLAs in the current legislature, it looks destined to disappear from the political landscape.

Social Organisations

The Young Mizo Association (YMA)

The YMA, which was founded in 1935, with a total membership of 145004 in 2003 in the northern zone alone, is still thriving. Its membership is open to both officials and non-officials. All political parties cultivate its support, though it has managed to remain to be seen as neutral and non-political. Its role in the preservation of traditional values and useful customs, and even in the maintenance of law and order is pivotal. Its approach to issues concerning the community is often conservative and at times tends to infringe on individual liberties.

Mizo Hmeichhe Insuihkhawm Pawl (MHIP)

This Association of Mizo Women was founded in the early 50s and has spread all over the state. Its available membership figure for the 5 districts of northern Mizoram in 2003 was 1,57,302, making it probably the largest NGO in India. Its motto is: To help others, though in the course of time, it has tended to concentrate on women issues. The YMA and MHIP are the two main NGOs, which are engaged in effective social work and charitable activities in the rural areas. As leaders of large and influential organizations, the leadership of these associations in the urban areas tends to waste time and energy in irrelevant popular activities.

Mizoram Upa Pawl (MUP) or Mizoram Senior Citizen's Association

Founded in the early 80s, the association in 2003 had 50400 members in the northern zone of Mizoram. The membership is open to men and women above the age of 50. Its aim is to preserve traditional values and to work for the welfare of senior citizens.

Mizo Zirlai Pawl (MZP) or Mizo Student's Association

The association was established in 1935 and has since gained preeminence as the forum of the youth. It was originally concerned with the interests and welfare of the Mizo students, especially in the endeavour to create understanding and unity among them. In addition, it has now transformed into a non-partisan political pressure group on various issues affecting not only the student community but also Mizoram as a whole. Its leaders have also increasingly used it as a staging ground for entry to full time participation in politics.

The Churches

The Mizos take pride in proclaiming that their community is 100 percent Christian. Christianity is indeed omnipresent in the life of the community. This is amply demonstrated by the fact that no community activities can commence without what is termed '*hunserh*,' a brief dedication service where some verses of the Bible is read, followed by a prayer for blessings on the particular activity of the occasion.

The established Churches are the Presbyterians in the north and the Baptists in the South. The Roman Catholic Church is also present and is slowly gaining adherents. There are a few other denominational groups with widely differing number of followers. The Churches organize their activities under various wings such as the youth, women, children and a common social front. In addition to the regular Church services, a number of camping crusades are held every year.

The liberal minded often allege that too much time is wasted on religious activities. The imposing presence of religion in the life of the community also appears to promote conformity while, in real terms, it does little to reform the daily lives of its adherents. As the result, uprightness in appearance and form without inner reform, indeed, hypocrisy seems to be slowly becoming a norm in Mizo society.

3. Economic Profile

The economic life of the Mizos has always been centered around *jhum* or shifting cultivation. During the rule of the Chiefs, the chiefs distributed jhum land every year from the land under their control to their subjects. The Village Councils now do the allocation of jhum land by letting the villagers draw lots. The sizes of the plots used to be usually between 1.5 and 3 hectares per family, depending on the number of able-bodied persons in a family. However, as land available for *jhuming* is becoming less due to allotment of lands to individuals, plot sizes in recent years have become smaller. Besides, the earning per man day in this practice of farming is so low that many young people now prefer to work as wage earners in services and other sectors.

Jhum sites selection is done in November/December and by mid February, felling of the vegetation is usually finished. The dried vegetation must be set on fire preferably before the early rains in mid March. After the unburned debris of trees and bamboos are cleared, the plot is ready for cultivation.

The crops grown in the plots are mixed. Paddy remains the principal crop and others that are inevitably grown are common vegetables and pulses for household consumption. Nowadays, cash crops such as ginger, turmeric, bird's eye chilly, oilseeds, maize, sugarcane, etc are grown. A variety of spices, herbs, flowers, fruits and oilseeds like sesame, soybeans and mustard and cotton can grow well in Mizoram. The basic problem is the method of farming the land, that is, the practice of shifting cultivation, which causes depletion of forests and biodiversity, soil erosion as also a complex of environmental damages. Crop yields from unleveled lands cannot be very high either. A new scientific thinking says that it is better to improve them through scientific methods than through replacement with plantations which represent an alien intrusion into a scientific pro-environmental as well as silk zone. It is important to better jhum, restrict its spread and involve micro-credit agencies and give better alternative markets. The jhumia is poor and marginalized. His work and that of his fellow—to be and improved. That lives and income grow, instead of condemning them with the prejudice of government and insensitive "encouragements". Alternative arrangements such as settled farming have not worked. This remains the basic task facing the governments that has yet to be structurally dealt with. Attempts to change the practice of jhuming through the programmes initiated by the Congress under the New Land Use Policy and by the present MNF government under the Mizoram Intodelh (Self Sufficiency) Project (MIP) have so far made no substantial difference.

Indicators of Current Status

The following selected facts and figures may help in assessing the current economic standing of Mizoram:

1. Population - 891058; females per 1000 males: 938; persons per square kilometer: 42; rural population: 53.9 per cent. (2001 Census).
2. Foodgrains production - paddy: 109,205 MT; maize: 14879 MT and pulses: 4986 MT. (2002-2003).

   (Update: 2007-08: paddy: 16688 MT, Maize 729 MT & Pulses : 2362MT)
3. Per capita income - Rs. 7517 (1993-94 in current prices).

   (Update: 2005-06: Rs. 23900) Compare this with an all India average of Rs. 7185.
4. Employment breakup - farmers (mainly *jhuming*) 66 per cent; manufacturing - 5 per cent and government employees, trading and services - 29 per cent.
5. Sources of the domestic product of the State - 40 per cent from farming, 15 per cent from manufacturing and 45 per cent from government employees, trading and services.
6. According to the central Planning Commission, those who were in 1993 below the poverty line (BPL) in Mizoram were 26 per cent (about 200000) whereas the State government reckoned it to be 56.07 per cent.
7. Literacy is 89.49 per cent as compared to all India's 52 per cent. While in literacy among the states of India Mizoram is placed second after Kerala, the drop out rate from Grades I - V in 1994-95 was 63 per cent. This clearly shows that the number of those who are able to go to High Schools is quite limited. For examples, in Aizawl District the number of enrolment in Primary Schools in 2001 was 33874, those who went

on to High Schools was 18389 and those went to Higher Secondary Schools was 5705. This is largely in an urban area where the schools are relatively well equipped with teaching staff and instruments. The corresponding figures for Champhai District, mostly rural area, are - Primary School, 14577, High School, 4947 and Higher Secondary School, 402. (Figures for the whole State are not yet available).

[Update : See page 37]

Resources

Mizoram has no known mineral resources, which are commercially exploitable. The few surveys that the Geological Survey of India and the Oil and Natural Gas Commission have conducted so far did not find any. In addition to human resources, the only natural resources of Mizoram are its fertile but fragile soil, forests, sub-tropical climatic condition in slopes of varied elevation and highly conducive to growth of various fruits, flowers and crops, and its numerous rivers. About these natural resources have already been detailed.

Infrastructure

As noted earlier, Mizoram is critically deficient in infrastructure development particularly in the physical kind. The few initiatives taken by the Sailo Ministry in 1979-84, especially in the power sector, have remained unimplemented. A brief account of what has been done in this sector will show the actual state of affairs.

Energy

The potential in this sector is enormous, particularly in the generation of electricity by means of the hydropower. Beside the active investigations that were conducted on hydropower projects such as Tuirial (60 MW), Tuivai (210 MW) and Serlui-B (12 MW), the Bairabi Hydel Project (120 MW) on the Tlawng or Daleshwari River had been ready for execution in the early 80s in the tenure of the Sailo Ministry.

The successor Ministries continued to ignore the project. It has now been revised with a reduced capacity of 80 MW. With the new policy of commercialization of large hydro projects in India, however, the State government faces a serious funding problem, unless the central government makes exception for Mizoram.

The North-East Electric Power Corporation (NEEPCO) has taken up Tuirial and Tuivai, but progress is slow. Only 12 percent of the electricity produced by these projects will be owned by the State and the rest of its requirement will have to be purchased. The Power Department is currently undertaking five Mini/Micro Hydel Projects: Tuirial-B (12 MW); Maicham (11MW); Tuipanglui (3 MW); Kau-Tlabung (3MW) and Lamsial (500 KW).

The Power Projects under investigation are: Kolodyne I - 120 MW (completed and pending for techno-economic clearance); Kolodyne II - 300 MW; Tuipui - 30 MW; Bairabi II - 50 MW; Tuichang - 30 MW; Tuirini - 60 MW and Tuivawl - 50 MW.

The current position regarding supply and consumption of electric power is:

Estimate of requirement: 102 MW as against existing supply of 72 MW; Electricity generated by the State: 22 MW (Diesel - 16 MW and Mini/Micro - 6 MW); Purchased from neighbouring States: 50 MW and shortage: 50 MW.

[Update: 2007-08: Installed: 37.17: Generation 366.34MW]

Transport System

The length of the network of roads in the State as on March 31, 2001 was 4122.37 kilometers, which included 328 kilometers of National Highways constructed and maintained by Border Road Organisation (BRO). Motorable roads connected 704 villages and the road length per 100 square kilometers was 19.54 km. (The Draft Five Year Plan for 2002 - 2007). Not only is construction of roads in the hilly terrains difficult, maintenance of these roads is extremely expensive. Often there are days when some areas remain inaccessible due to blockage of roads by landslides or other damages caused by heavy rains. Except for the National Highways and a few leading roads, much of the road length in Mizoram is unusable for load bearing heavy vehicles.

The main supply route for Mizoram is the National Highway-54 from Silchar in Assam to Aizawl and beyond. If this road is blocked even for a few days, many consumer goods become scarce. The other roads linking Mizoram with Manipur and Tripura are not yet pliable by heavy vehicles on a regular basis. Even otherwise, these States cannot supply the requirements of Mizoram as they are equally remote from the centers of manufactured goods as Mizoram is.

Mizoram's hilly terrain limits the scope of rail and air links. There are not many stretches of level land where long runways can be made. On December 12, 1998, the first airport was opened at Lengpui, near Aizawl, where medium-sized jet aircraft can land and take off. No facilities for transportation of air cargo are available yet. Nor is there any night landing facility. The entire airport building is over-large, over-expensive and underutilized. It is another example of the Center's partnership with local authorities without a proper cost-benefit analysis. The only rail link to Mizoram is by a narrow gauge railroad, which terminated at Bairabi, a town situated at the bank of Daleshwari, 3 km. from Assam border. Surprisingly, the urgency of development and expansion of this lone rail link does not seem to register with the present authorities.

Two Inland Waterways, on the Karnafuli river between Chittagong and Demagiri in Mizoram and on the Daleshwari river, that were in much use during the British rule became virtually unused after the partition of India. After the construction of the Kaptai Dam on the Karnafuli in Bangladesh, a huge area around Demagiri has been submerged. This created a good potential for inland water transport in the area, provided understanding in the matter can be reached between the governments of Bangladesh and India. The Tlawng or Daleshwari joins the Barak in Cachar and was used by the Mizos for travel and transportation down to areas, which have become Bangladesh, and even to Shillong and the plains of Assam in India. Except for floating down forest produce like bamboo and timber, Mizoram hardly uses this route any more, perhaps, due to uncertain transit facilities beyond Cachar.

The Barak river and a long stretch of its tributary, Tuivai, was also much used by the inhabitants of northeast Mizoram and the southeast area of Manipur for supply and travel route. Due to insurgent activities across the rivers on the Manipur side, the use of these waterways has become erratic. The Kolodyne in South Mizoram can also, perhaps, be harnessed for transit to Akyab in Myanmar, once the projected hydro dams on it are constructed.

Yet 4.7 million Rupees was earmarked for development of inland water-ways in the plan for 2002-2007-a reflection of poor planning and perception and especially when one consider the huge investment in air links.

[Update: upto 2008 PWD National Highway: 328.00 Km: State Highway: 699.79 km; Project Pushpak Road 1558.44 Km.]

Communications

As the network of post offices depends for the dispatch of mails on the physical transport system, its services are relatively slow. Non-courier mails from Delhi take a week or more to reach Aizawl while Speed Post takes about 3 to 4 working days. The population per Post Office in 1993-94 was 1920. As of June 2003, there were nine telephone exchanges in Mizoram with working connections in the Secondary Switching Area, numbering 54255 subscribers. The telephone equipment currently has the capacity for 73120 connections. Mizoram is now linked by an underground optic fibre wires. The telecom system still does not have the capacity for information highway. During the year preceding June 2003, 1027 new Internet connections were provided.

[Update: 2008: 360 Branches of Post Office: 60; Telephone Exchanges: Mobile Phones Subscribers : BSNL: 55594; AIR TEL: 121869; RELIANCE: 79300; AIRCEL : 28509]

Water Supply

Water supply during the dry season has always been a special problem of Mizoram. The villages were traditionally situated on hilltops, as a part of the strategy for defence against on coming enemies. The practice has still continued. Thus, the only viable way to provide water supply to these settlements is to pump river water to a reservoir located on a high point above the settlements and distribute the water by gravity. This is being done for the urban areas and some selected villages. With the chronic shortage of electric power supply, it will be a long way before adequate supply of water, if at all, can be arranged for the people of Mizoram.

The Department of Public Health Engineering, which is responsible for water supply and sanitation, also promotes tapping of underground water by means of hand pumps. A number of these pump sets have been distributed yearly. With severe depletion of underground water during dry season, this is a poor supplement to water supply work. Harvesting of rainwater is a practice long known in Mizoram. Since there is usually excess of rainwater during the rainy season, with improved collection, storage and distribution facilities, rainwater can be gainfully harvested and substantially augment the water supply during the dry season. The government of Mizoram has yet take meaningful initiatives in this direction.

Human Resources

The department of School Education and that of the Higher and Technical Education are in charge of human resource development. Like in the rest of India, a scheme for quality education for all (Sarva Shiksha Abhyian) was introduced in 2003 in Mizoram. Under this scheme, all children in the age group of 6 to 14 years are expected to attend school. In 2003, there were 8,985 out of school children from this age group as compared to 17,993 in 2002, representing a signal progress. For the age group of 15 to 35 years, a new project called 'Eradication of Residual Illiteracy' (ERIP) has been introduced. With the implementation of these two projects, the State expects to achieve full literacy by 2007.

The main weakness of the education system has been the continuing lack of technical equipment and quality staff for science and technical education at the school level. This has cumulatively resulted in a very low proportion of scientists and technologists among the educated Mizos. There is also a distinct lack of what might be termed 'scientific temper' among the intellectuals. At present, except for veterinary sciences, there is no degree level school for engineering or medical subjects. The Mizoram University, which opened in 2001, has not been able to introduce courses in physical sciences.

The present position of educational institutions in Mizoram follows:

Primary Schools: 1225; Middle Schools: 777; High Schools: 408; Colleges: 30; Polytechnics: 2; Teachers Training Institutes: 2; University: 1. There is a University of Veterinary Sciences run by the central government. There is also a Regional Institute for Nursing, Laboratory Technicians and Pharmacology owned by the North-East Council (NEC). There are a few departmentally managed, diploma levels, vocational training institutes for information technology, mechanics, etc.

[Update: 2007-08: University: 1; Student: 1988; College, Including Law Collage: 22; Student: 5465; Training Institutes:

15; Student: 4309; Hihger Secondary School: 82; Student: 12816; High School: 508; Student: 43675; Middle School: 1090; Student: 57399; Primary School: 1752; Student: 134656].

Public Health

In terms of persons per public health care establishments, Mizoram may have the most health care facilities among the States of India. With 14 hospitals in the State, the number of persons per hospital bed in 1991 was already 627, the lowest among the northeast States. The next lowest, Arunachal's was 755 as compared to all India for 1324 persons. But this is about quantity, not quality. The main problem affecting the health care system in Mizoram, like in education, is the lack of equipment, medicines and specialists, compounded by erratic and fluctuating electric power supply. Without adequate diagnostic, radiological and other laboratory facilities, the most competent physician cannot be effective.

Because of this persisting problem, most patients with complicated cases, especially those who require sophisticated surgery, had to be referred to private medical institutions outside Mizoram in such places as Guwahati, Kolkata, Vellore, Chennai, Delhi and Bombay. This not only creates easily avoidable hardships for the people, but is also a serious drain on the finances of the State since so many of its employees undergo medical treatment outside the State. The fact that patients who need bandages or syringes have often to buy them from private suppliers outside the hospital amply demonstrates the seriousness of the situation.

The government is currently constructing a hospital designed to serve as Referral Hospital, to be so equipped and staffed as to obviate the necessity of sending patients to places outside the State. With the basic foundation of the health care system in disarray as it is now, it is doubtful if the government will be competent enough to manage such a hospital.

The number of health care centers managed by the government are as follows:

Subsidiary Health Centers: 351; Primary Health Centers: 58.

[Update: 2007: Hospital: Nos. 10; Beds 944; Community Health Centre: Nos 9; bed: 270; Primary Health Centre : Nos. 57; Beds: 570; Sub Centre: Nos. 366].

Banking and Finance

The common people in Mizoram seldom use banking instruments for their financial transactions. They mostly use cash money. Those who use banks do it mainly for saving or term deposits. Taking loans from banks against collaterals is also popular. The number of 'bad loans' is said to be high, particularly those loans extended by the first financial institution set up by the State, Zoram Industrial Development Corporation (ZIDCO).

ZIDCO was set up by the State government in collaboration with the Industrial Development Bank of India (IDBI) to foster the start up and the growth of industries in Mizoram. Another semi-financial institution, Mizoram Khadi and Village Industries Board (KVI) in 1986, was set up to promote various types of small scale and cottage industries. These two institutions extend credits to individuals and cooperative bodies for starting small industries. Part of the funding for the loans they service comes from the central credit institutions for development.

There are two central government sponsored financial institutions, North Eastern Development Finance Corporation (NEDFI) and National Bank for Agriculture and Rural Development (NABARD), which have recently opened branch offices in Mizoram with junior official representatives. These two have yet to make substantial contribution to the development of Mizoram. Full fledged banks that are operating in Mizoram are: State Bank of India (SBI); Vijayya Bank; United Commercial Bank; Mizoram Cooperative Apex Bank; Mizoram Rural Bank and Mizoram Urban Cooperative Bank. The Credit-Deposit ratio in 1996 was 16.

[Update: 2008: SBI: UCO: VIJAYA: IDBI: UBI:AXIS: SYNSICATE:CBI:BOB:PNB:MCAB:MRB:MUCO: Total Branches: 108: Total Deposit: Rs. in crores 1668.05 Total Advances: 990.82: C: D Ratio 5940].

The banks in Mizoram were not authorized to deal in foreign currency exchange until recently. The State Bank of India is now authorized to do so.

Selected Economic Sectors with Prospects

1. Agriculture

The major agricultural crops, total yield for each crop in 2002-2003 in metric tons, and the area sown in hectares are given below:

Paddy (jhum):	67,076: 41,356;		
WRC:	33,725: 12,905;	HYV: 8,404: 2,806.	
Maize:	14,879: 7,489;	Pulses:	4,986: 4,666;
Oilseeds:	5,285: 7,132;	Tapioca:	1,330: 232;
Sugarcane:	7,443: 1,370;	Potato:	726: 369.

As already explained elsewhere, shifting cultivation of rice is uneconomic and has no future. Alternative crops that have already been identified as suitable for Mizoram, especially horticultural crops, must be encouraged.

[Update : 2007-08Production in 2008-2009 in matric tons and sown in hecters.

Paddy (jhum): 68917: 51990;
Maize: 9318: 9558;
Oilseeds: 2514: 2275;
Pulses: 3646: 3931;
Sugarcane: 13696: 1342;
Potato: 1569: 269].

2. *Horticulture*

Production in 2002-2003	*Area in Ha.*	*Production: MT*
1. Fruits	21,150	57,858
2. Plantation Crops	3,478	6,844
3. Vegetables	7,581	40,970
4. Spices	7,058	36,439
5. Roots & Tubers	850	5,286.

Systematic promotion of horticulture in Mizoram is recent, although plantation of fruits like orange, hatkora (of citrus family) and pineapples has been in long practice. Mizoram has been identified to be ideal for a variety of horticultural crops. The State government is now making a thrust in this sector. The crops with potential are briefly described in the following:

A. *Fruits*: Grape: Bangalore Blue is cultivated in an area of about 1,000 Ha. in the eastern high altitude area. The yield is 70-80 quintal/acre. Passion Fruit: Cultivated so far in about 2,000 hectares, it is said to grow well again the eastern region. Orange: Mandarin was popular but has declined owing to disease. It is being revived with improved seedlings. Banana - growing is getting large scale and is now marketed in Meghalaya and Assam. The variety of banana grown in Mizoram is perhaps the best in the world.

B. *Spices*: Turmeric - Lakadang variety as well as the traditional turmeric, native to the place, grows well. The native turmeric called 'Ai-ong' can grow as shrubs in wooded sites and can be left wild for a few years. Its roots do not deteriorate but multiply and the quality appears to improve. Promotion of this crop is at the initial stage. Only 2785 MT was harvested in 2002-2003. Ginger - has been increasingly grown, but with frequent price fluctuation, its prospect is uncertain. It also causes serious soil erosion. In 2002-2003, 47,821 MT was harvested. (This was obviously not included in the spices production listed herein earlier). Chillies - a variety of chillies has been grown. Bird's Eye chilly is indigenous to Mizoram and is the most sought after for export.

C. *Plantation*: Arecanut - is grown in the western and northwestern lowlands. It does not yet meet local consumption.

D. *Flowers*: Rose- grows well and has good prospects but not enough yet for export outside the State. Anthurium - was tried for mass production only in 2002. It is already sold as cut flower in metropolis of other States. It can be harvested in 10 months and appears to be better in quality than those grown in other States. Bird-of-Paradise (BOP) - was introduced two years ago. It was expected to flower in 3 years, but has done so this year. It seems to have a bright future.

Other varieties of horticultural crop being tried are black pepper, cardamom, jatropha carcus, vanilla, etc. Medicinal herbs, native to Mizoram, have also yet to be identified and the case of growing others to be explored.

[Update : Production in 2008-2009 Area in Ha.Production in MT:]

1. Fruits	26,600:	9,193.5:
2. Plantation Crops:	8,507:	10,072:
3 .Vegetables:	3,527:	3,527:
4. Spices:	28,751:	6,000:
5. Medicinal Plants:	1,525:	721.5:
6. Flowers:	233	23,00,000: no.
7. Turmeric:	9,625:	39,862.5:
8. Ginger:	10,391:	34,290:
9. Bird's Eye chilly	7,185:	14,429:
Anthurium:	26 Ha:	75lac.
Rose:	6 Ha:	27lac.

3. *Forest-Based Industry*

Apart from processing horticultural crops when it has in optimum quantities, the most suitable industrial sector for Mizoram appears to be forest-based. Bamboo in particular is plentiful and is easily renewable. At present, due to the shortage of electric power, large-scale industrial plants cannot be set up.

4. Others

In 2002, there were 1500 cottage and small-scale industries operating and producing goods worth Rs. 370.5 million. There were 4258 registered small industries in 2003. (Mid Term Appraisal of Five-Year Plan). Animal Husbandry, Fishery, Sericulture and Tourism sectors are not yet in the take-off stage.

[Update: : Registered during 2007-08: Small Scale Industries: 205 : Employed Persons : 594: Investment: 593 Rs. in Lakhs]

Tourism, however, seems to have a good potential, if international standard infrastructure and facilities can be provided. Mizoram can be projected as a unique and exotic tourist destination.

4. Relations with Neighbouring States

Apart from the inter-States interactions initiated by the North Eastern Council (NEC), the present political leadership of Mizoram does not maintain much interaction with its neighbours. This may be partly because the current party in power, the MNF, is a regional party with no direct links to other parties. However, with several problems in common with the other States in the region, such as security, law and order, infrastructure needs, health care, etc., close coordination with them cannot but be useful.

Relations with Assam

One outstanding problem with Assam is the issue of the northern boundary of Mizoram with the Cachar District of

Assam. The present demarcation was specified by Section 6 of the North Eastern Areas (Reorganisation) Act, 1971. Vide Section 4.2 (1) of the Peace Accord signed with the Government of India in 1986 the MNF Party accepted it. And the then Congress government of Mizoram countersigned the Accord, implying that the State government also accepted it. The MNF and the Congress are the only two political parties, which came into power after the 1986 Accord. Since their hands are tied by the Accord they had signed, they are not in a position to dispute the boundary arrangement.

However, from the time of the Mizo District Council in the 1950s till the early 1980s, the authorities in Mizoram as well as the general public had been objecting to what was fixed first as the de facto boundary of the then District and later of the Union Territory of Mizoram. The UT government even constituted a 'Fact Finding Committee' in 1973 on the matter. The 'Summary Finding' of that committee stated, "The Mizos are unsatisfied with the line and manner in which their Northern Boundary with Cachar was fixed arbitrarily by the British and are likely to remain so for generations to come, unless and until it is refixed based on certain reasonable grounds like historical, traditional and occupational backgrounds. From the study of the boundary fixation herein related, it is clear that there was such a line and in its final form is represented by the Inner Line of 1875."

This is not a live political issue at present, but the general public has still not accepted the boundary. NGOs like YMA and MZP have been keeping the issue alive by raising it in public and the media. And the State government may one day be forced to dispute the boundary in the future.

Under the existing Inner Line regulations, Indians other than Mizos as well as foreigners are required to obtain Inner Line Permit (ILP) before entering Mizoram. There is therefore no problem of migration from Assam into Mizoram. There is, however, a large floating population of masonries, carpenters and construction workers from Assam, particularly the Kaimganj area of Cachar, scattered all over Mizoram. Some who came without ILP or overstayed their Permit or commit crime are occasionally deported by the authorities.

As Mizoram's entire supply of manufactured and essential goods and construction materials comes from or through Assam, it cannot afford to disrupt its relationship with Assam. No trade figures are available, as interstate trades are not recorded. The entire surplus of cash crop produces of Mizoram, such as chilies, ginger, cotton, oilseeds and other product like orange and grapefruits are sold to Cachar. Way back in 1994, a group called 'Hnam Chhantu' (a group campaigning for self reliance for Mizoram) conducted a research on the extent of the dependence of Mizoram on food products of Assam. The food items selected were vegetables, cooking oil, fish and eggs. They found that the city of Aizawl alone consumed these items in one month, which cost at the time over Rs. 28 million.

Relations with Manipur

Mizo tribes or people of Mizo origin inhabit the southern and western hill areas and some parts of the northern region of Manipur. These people freely come and go. As insurgent groups have been active in these hills areas, a number of people from the area, especially the South District of Manipur, fleeing from the disturbed area, have been migrating to Mizoram. The migrants are largely accommodated and face no difficulty in integrating into the society. A National Highway from Aizawl crosses into the southeast of Manipur and there are thrice weekly flights of Indian Airlines between Aizawl and Imphal. There is a steady flow of people on both sides.

Two small insurgent outfits, based in Manipur, are occasionally active in the northern part of Mizoram. The Zomi Revolutionary Army (ZRA) claims to work for the reunification of what it terms 'Zomis' or tribes of Zo origin and is active in the Paite inhabited area of northeast Mizoram. The Hmar People Convention (Democratic) or HPC (D) demands the curving of Hmar Autonomous District Council in the Hmar tribe occupied area of mid north Mizoram and occasionally launches its activities either from Cachar Hills of Assam or southwest Manipur. Their leader, Lalhmingthang, hailed from Khawlian village of Mizoram and now usually resides at Lakhipur in Cachar District. The ZRA personnel are mostly drawn from Paites of south Manipur while those of the HPC (D) is a mixture of Hmars from Manipur and Mizoram. Some times, the insurgents of the Manipur valley, the Meiteis, also cross over to northern Mizoram and encounter the security forces.

The Nagas demand the integration of all the Naga inhabited areas of India. If this is agreed to by the Government of India, a large chunk of northern Manipur will have to be integrated into Nagaland. In that event, the Mizo tribes of southern Manipur are likely to fight for incorporation into Mizoram. The Meitei insurgents foresee this and are steadily asserting their writ over the area. This is a possible future issue that can seriously complicate the relationship between Manipur and Mizoram.

Relations with Tripura

Mizoram and Tripura are, perhaps, the least interactive of neighbours. Some 7000 Brus, a non-Mizo ethnic group, fled from western Mizoram to Tripura in 1998 and are now encamped as refugees in two locations there. They are being looked after by the central government, though their presence could strain the services sector in the area. The refugees claim that the Mizos tried to force them to convert into Christianity and that they had to flee Mizoram for fear of being persecuted. The Mizos amongst whom the Brus had lived and the State government vehemently denied this. They in turn claim that false rumours spread by vested interest working against Christianity in Mizoram alarmed the Brus and they migrated to Tripura of their own accord. During the last election to the Legislative Assembly of Mizoram in November 2003, there was an unsuccessful attempt by the Opposition parties and some NGOs to block the postal ballots cast by these refugees.

The Tripura Chief Minister alleged in 2003 that there were some training camps in Mizoram of the insurgent groups fighting against his government such as the All Tripura People's Liberation Organisation and the All Tripura Tiger Force. Given the mobility of the mostly hill men fighters operating against the Tripura government and their familiarity with the jungles of the 66 km. long border with Mizoram, it is quite possible that they sometimes set up shelters on the Mizoram side of the border. The present Chief Minister of Mizoram, Zoramthanga, a former rebel leader, has often been accused by the Opposition Parties of secretly enlisting the support of insurgents such as HPC (D) and ZRA and of abetting the transportation of weapons by the National Socialist Council of Nagaland (Isaac-Muivah) or NSCN (I-M) through Mizoram. These accusations have not been proved or conclusively substantiated, as there has not been constituted a formal enquiry to look into these matters.

Across the state boundary in Tripura is the Jampui Hills range, which is peopled by the Mizos in about a dozen villages. These people look towards Mizoram for their cultural succour. A number of the educated among them migrated to Mizoram and some of them occupy high official posts. They make no political demand and provide a potential useful bridge between the two States, though they have not been used as such so far.

There is no direct air link with Tripura. Two fairly good roads link the two States. There are markets along the road across Kanhmun (Mizoram) on both sides of the border. Some manufactured goods of daily needs and local agricultural products are traded in these markets. Some goods smuggled from Bangladesh especially processed baby foods and used clothes pass into Mizoram at this border. The trade between the two States is negligible.

External Relations

Relations with Bangladesh

In the scheme with which India has so far conducted its

relationship with Bangladesh, the interests of the Northeast States, particularly of Mizoram, do not seem to figure prominently. (A copy of declassified Note on Indo-Bangladesh Relations is at Appendix G). This is perhaps due to the fact that the spirit and the level of bilateral cooperation have not attained the stage where detailed sub-regional concerns can be accommodated. It can also be because the Mizoram government has not made concrete structural proposals to the Government of India for beneficial relationship between the State and Bangladesh.

Some officials and non-official trade representatives including the Chief Minister have recently made visits to Bangladesh with the ostensible purpose of improving the officially non-existent trading relations. Without agreed border trade posts and transit arrangements at the level of the two national governments, and improved land transport system in the border areas, there can be no meaningful trade exchanges between Mizoram and Bangladesh. The manner in which India pursues its relations with Myanmar (noted hereinafter) clearly attests to this. The political leadership in Mizoram sometimes spoke of proposals for setting up border trade posts along the border with Bangladesh. But such proposals do not figure in the notes of the Ministry responsible for the conduct of India's external relations.

As noted earlier, inland water transport and border trade posts, to begin with, can be easily arranged on the Karnafuli River and the Kaptai dam area in the south. What is missing appears to be close coordination by the State government with the central government. Small scale informal trade does exist in the area, with mainly bamboos and some agricultural products going into Bangladesh while fish and some merchandises come from there.

Except for a few underground Bru or Tuikuk volunteers, who are demanding a separate administrative arrangement for themselves in the northwestern area of Mizoram, the border area is largely free of insurgents. As the border with Bangladesh can be freely crossed in all seasons, however, migration from Bangladesh, particularly of the Chakmas, has long been a problem disturbing the Mizos. During the British rule and after Indian independence till 1954, the Standing Orders issued by the successive Superintendents of Lushai (Mizo) Hills District specified the Chakmas as foreigners and they were required to obtain permits to work in Mizoram. The Chakma tribe was also not listed among the minority tribes in the Indian Constitution at the time of its adoption. In the 1941 Census, there were 18 Chakmas in Mizoram and their number shot up to 15,297 in 1951. By 1971, when the Parliament passed the North-Eastern Areas (Reorganisation) Act (NEAR Act), they became so numerous that the Government of India decided to set up the Chakma Autonomous District Council within Mizoram.

No public protest was orchestrated against the creation of Chakma District at the time. The then District Council formed by the Congress had not objected to the proposed NEAR Act; and on October 2, 1971 the General Assembly of the Mizo Union also accepted it. The PC party started the campaign against what it termed as the unjust creation of an administrative district for foreigners. Upon coming into power in 1979, the PC government headed by Brig. T. Sailo prepared plans to differentiate genuine Indian Chakmas, who entered Mizoram before January 26, 1952 from those Chakma foreigners who came after the adoption of Indian Constitution. It proposed to expel the latter, but could not execute its plans as the government was voted out in the 1984 election. In 1986, three MLAs from the PC party tabled a draft resolution in the State Assembly, proposing the dissolution of the Chakma Autonomous District Council. The MNF and the Congress combine voted against it and defeated it. (Proceedings of the 6th Session of the Fourth Legislative Assembly of Mizoram - pp.161). Since then, the Chakma issue has been kept alive of and on mainly by the MZP. Political parties also often rake it up during election years. The population of Chakma District as per 2001 Census was 34,528.

Relations with Myanmar

Mizoram does not maintain direct political relationship with Myanmar, as the subject is the concern of the central government in Delhi. However, the Government of India conducts its relationship with the Myanmar regime, essentially with a view to promote and safeguard the interests of the Northeast States especially those bordering Myanmar. Without the active cooperation of the Myanmar authorities, India is clearly aware, the major problems of the Northeast, namely insurgency, underdevelopment, drugs and arms smuggling cannot be eliminated. A number of agreements that India has concluded as also its proposed projects with Myanmar clearly attest to this. Officials of the State government have invariably included in the Indian delegations when such delegations are mandated to discuss matters concerning the respective Northeast States. As a democracy, India is naturally bound to favour a democratic Myanmar, but its vital interests compel active cooperation with whatever regime that country has. A copy of a declassified Note on Indo-Myanmar Relations is at Appendix H.

The major project proposals that concerns Mizoram are India's offer to upgrade Rhi-Tiddim and Rhi-Falam roads linking Mizoram with Chin State, setting up of border trade post at Zokhawthar-Rhi and the Kolodyne or Kaladan Multimodal Project for a combination of inland water transport and highway linking southern Mizoram to Rakhine. These projects and other ideas of infrastructure links were already initiated during the time when the present writer was Indian Ambassador to Myanmar in the mid 1990s. It was however not possible to take them up quickly as the Myanmar authorities were at times frustratingly cautious and slow to respond. The bridge on the border river, Tiao, and a smaller one farther into Myanmar were constructed by India in that time, though. The same Mizo ethnic groups inhabit the entire regions adjoining Mizoram on the Myanmar side. And, perhaps, this is part of the reason that makes Myanmar cautious. The presence of some Chin pro-democracy activists in Mizoram and the fact that the Chin insurgents (the Chin National Army) have occasionally taken shelters inside Mizoram have not helped matters.

Though the border trade post is yet to be officially opened, the age-old traditional informal trade goes merrily on. Sources in the Customs authorities indicated that the goods "seized" during the last three years were: 2000-2001: Rs. 13.2 million; 2002-2003: Rs. 17.6 million; 2003-2004: Rs. 38.6 million. These are supposed to be the costs of goods confiscated and sold in auction by the Customs. Except for narcotics and arms, real seizures are rare and so are real auctions. Except for trade in head loads of local produces within 30 kilometers on both sides of the border, the entire trade is illegal. And the Customs officials are supposed to seize all goods that come from Myanmar. However, this is not the case in reality. In the assessment of knowledgeable circles, the above figures should represent only 40 per cent of the trade or even less.

The main items of trade that come from Myanmar are: kitchen wares and gadgets; entertainment electronics like TVs, Hi-fi sets, radios; watches; electric goods; garments and other textile products; jewelries including unworked gold and precious stones; furniture and carpentry tools; etc. Light goods and not so light goods like refrigerators and washing machines that a household needs are all available. Vendors often sell them from house to house. The products smuggled are mostly made in China, Japan, S. Korea, Thailand and Taiwan.

The goods that enter Myanmar have been estimated by the Customs to cost about the same as those that come from there. These are mainly Indian made products such as light building materials like kitchen and bathroom fittings and fixtures, bicycles and spare parts, sewing machines, all kinds of pharmaceutical products including proxyvon (which is abused), finished leather products, textiles (loin cloth pieces), plastics and linoleum products, etc. Much of the smuggled drugs and pharmaceuticals is said to reach southern China.

Once legal border trade posts are established on both sides of the border and the roads across Mizoram are improved, the volume of trade exchanges is likely increase substantially. Then, there will have been an official channel that can be abused.

A large number of Myanmar "guest workers" (considering the size of Mizoram population) are in the State. Apart from a few handloom weavers from the plains of Myanmar, most of these workers are from the Chin Hills, who can become fluent in Mizo language in a matter of weeks as they belong to the same ethnic group. They are mainly engaged in menial jobs like housemaids, gardeners, drivers, farm workers and daily labours while a few are in trading and services. Before 2003, their number hovered around 40,000, about 5 per cent of the State population. In late 2003, an incident of rape of a minor girl committed by one of them triggered a widespread protest and a large number were forced to leave Mizoram, thereby attracting adverse comments even by the UN Human Rights Commission and the Amnesty International.

The State government has since started registering these workers and regulating the duration of their stay. Their number is said to have dwindled somewhat. However, the registration is done only at Zokhawthar-Rhi whereas the porous border can be crossed and is crossed at several points in the dry season. International agencies tend to regard these workers as victims of political oppression. They are more of 'economic migrants', some temporary, some not so, much like the Bangladeshis moving into India by various means elsewhere.

Regional Cooperation

Situated on the northeast end of the country, Mizoram is among the remotest of outposts in the North East. If the Partition put back the economy of the NER by a quarter-century, as reckoned by B. G. Verghese, (India's Northeast Resurgent, 1996), it must have put back the economy of

Mizoram at least by half a century. The Partition completely cut off its main traditional market, now Bangladesh, and rendered its only inland waterways, the Karnafuli and the Daleshwari, useless. Its only fragile link to the rest of the world became by a mountainous fair weather road from Cachar to Aizawl, which was subjected to frequent blockages by landslides during the rains. Though this road has been much improved and became a National Highway, it remains the main supply line for Mizoram. Fifty-seven years after Independence, the isolation of Mizoram is still acute.

In order to break out of its isolation, it is an absolute must for Mizoram to have access not only to a network of transport systems but also to other infrastructure linkages in the NER and beyond. The proposed or existing Asian Highways (AH) and the Trans-Asian Railways (TAR) systems do not include Mizoram. It seems to remain a "forgotten patch" of geography. Without access to the regional or sub-regional transport systems, it will obviously not be able to benefit from the regional cooperation intended by such groups as the Bay of Bengal Initiatives on Multi-sector, Technical and Economic Cooperation, the South Asian Development Quadrangle and the Kunming Initiatives.

Following are a layman's suggestions to give additional connectivity to Bangladesh while providing Mizoram the much-needed integration to the regional network of transportation:

1. While the proposed diversion of AH from Sylhet - Karimganj (Assam) - Silchar - Jiribam - Imphal -Tamu (Myanmar) may still stand, the existing road link from Agartala - Aizawl - Champhai (Mizoram) - Tiddim or Falam (Myanmar) can be extended to AH either in Bangladesh at Sylhet itself or in Cachar (Assam). This will also bring Tripura, Mizoram and Chin Hills, all underdeveloped States, into the AH network. The immediate advantage is that there are no insurgent activities anywhere along this road whereas Jiribam -

Imphal section of the other route is in the middle of insurgent area. The sections in Mizoram and Chin Hills in Myanmar pass through hilly terrains but can be upgraded without much difficulty, as they are essential supply lines constantly in use. Government of India has already offered to upgrade Rhi - Tiddim and Rhi - Falam roads.

2. Linking Chittagong by Highway-cum-Inland Waterway via Kaptai dam and Demagiri (Mizoram) to the proposed Multi-Modal Highway-cum-IWT Project on the Kaladan through the existing road in Mizoram from Lunglei to Saiha is another possibility. Another road can also be constructed in south Mizoram to link with the proposed Chittagong - Yangon road, which is already in advanced stage of construction.

3. Once transit through Bangladesh by rail and road to Kolkata is possible, linking the existing network of roads in the middle section of Mizoram will not be difficult.

4. If Tripura is linked by rail across Akhaura in Bangladesh, the same can be extended to the proposed Hydel Project at Bairabi in Mizoram by road-cum-rail, thereby extending farther into Mizoram via IWT.

5. Linking Jiribam by rail or road or both to the proposed Hydel Project at Tipaimuk on the Barak River may also be feasible. This again will provide IWT links to the interior of both Manipur and Mizoram.

REFERENCES

1. Biakchhunga, former Army Chief and President, MNF, *Nation Building* (Hnam Kalsiam - Mizo), 1996, Mizoram Publication Board.

2. Centre for Monitoring Indian Economy, *Basic Statistics Relating to Indian Economy*, Bombay.

3. Centre for Northeast Studies and Policy Research, *India's Northeast & Bangladesh, Problems & Opportunities*, 2004.

4. Comptroller and Auditor General of India, *Reports on Government*

of Mizoram, Shillong.

5. Deputy Commissioner of Customs, Aizawl.

6. Government of Mizoram, Mid Term Appraisal for Tenth Five Year Plan (2002-2007); Draft Tenth Five Year Plan (2002-2007); Annual Report of Environment and Forests Department (2003); Statistical Abstract of Department of Agriculture & Minor Irrigation; 30 Years of Mizoram Assembly; Unpublished Manuscript on Mizoram Economy and The Development of Mizoram in the Last 4 Years (2003) by the Directorate of Information & Public Relation; Extracts from Draft Annual Plan of Horticulture Department for 2005 by courtesy of Samuel Rosanglura, Director of the Department, *Statistical Handbook*, 2003; Extracts from the Records of Planning Cell of the Public Works Department (PWD) - courtesy of Mr. Sanghrima, Executive Engineer, etc.

7. Institute of Developing Economies, Japan, Sub-Regional Relations In The Eastern South Asia: With Special Focus on Bangladesh and Bhutan by Kyoko Inoue, Mayumi Murayama, M. Rahmatullah and Centre for Bhutan Studies, 2004.

8. Keivom, L., Zoram Khawvel - I (The World of Zoram -Mizo), M.C. Lalrinthanga, 1992. Aizawl.

9. Lalthanliana, Dr., *Mizo History – Before 1900* (Mizo), 2000, Aizawl.

10. Lalthangliana, B., *The History of Mizos – In India, Burma & Bangladesh* (Mizo), Remkungi, 2001, Aizawl.

11. Ministry of External Affairs, Government of India: *Notes on Indo-Myanmar Relations and Indo-Bangladesh Relations*. Personal interviews were conducted with Mrs. Neelam Deo, Joint Secretary (BSM), Mrs. Mitra Vashisht, Joint Secretary (SEA-I) and Mr. Lal Dingliana, Joint Secretary (FSI & Technical Cooperation).

12. NEC, *Basic Statistics of Northeast Region,* 1998, Shillong.

13. Pudaite, L. T., Personal data bank based on materials collected in the process of extensive travel on both sides of the Indo-Myanmar border, experience and reports sent to Government of India as Indian Ambassador to Myanmar (1995-96) and later as a freelance writer. The sources cannot now be listed as no record of references was made at the time.

14. Ray, Animesh, *Mizoram, India - Land and the People* Series, 1993, National Book Trust, New Delhi.

15. Sailo, Brig. T., *A Soldier's Story*, Cambridge Laser Print, 2001, Calcutta.

16. Sing Khaw Khai, Zo People and Their Culture, Khampu Hatzaw, Lamka, Mainpur, 1995.

17. Vanlalchhawna, Dr., *Zofate Economy (Economy of the Zos* - Mizo), Zamzo Publishing House, Aizawl, 2004.

18. Verghese, B.G., *India's Northeast - Resurgent*, Konark Publishers (Pvt) Ltd., 1996.

19. Vumson, *Zo History*, Author, Aizawl,

20. Zakhuma, Dr. K.M., *Political Development in Mizoram from 1946 to 1989*, Mizoram Publication Board, 2001.

APPENDIX - A

Table 1
Rivers in Mizoram

Sl. No.	*Name of river*	*Length in Kilometer (in Mizoram)*
1.	Tlawng (Dhaleshwari)	185.15
2.	Tiak	159.39
3.	Chhimtuipui (Kolodyne)	130.46
4.	Khawthlangtuipui (Karnaphuli)	128.08
5.	Tuichang	120.75
6.	Tuirial (Sonai)	117.53
7.	Tuichawng	107.87
8.	Mat	90.16
9.	Tuipui (Khawchhak)	86.94
10.	Tuivawl	72.45
11.	Teirei	70.84
12.	Tuirini	59.57
13.	Serlui	56.35

Note: Tui in Mizo language means water.

Table 2: Hill Ranges and Peaks in Mizoram

Name of Range/Peak	*Height(in metre)*
1. Blue Mountain (Phawngpui)	2,157
2. Lengteng	2,141
3. Surtlang	1,967
4. Lurhtlang	1,935
5. Tantlang	1,929
6. Vapartlang	1,897
7. Chalfithlang	1,866
8. Hranturotlang	1,854
9. Zopuitlang	1,850
10. Tawitlang	1,837
11. Mawmrangtlang	1,812
12. Puruntlang	1,758
13. Hmuifangtlang	1,619
14. Saireptlang	1,555
15. Sakawrhmuituaitlang	1,535
16. Reiktlang	1,485
17. Thorantlang	1,387
18. Buia Hmuntlang(Aizawl)	1,383
19. Serkawn (Lunglei)	1,222
20. Laipuitlang (Aizawl)	1,188
21. South Hlimentlang (Aizawl)	1,179

Note: Tlang in Mizo Language mean hills.

APPENDIX - B

GEOMORPHOLOGY, GEOLOGY, STRAITIGRAPHY, MINERALS ETC. OF MIZORAM

Geomorphology

As the terrain is very immature in response to recent tectonism, topographical features show prominent relief. The major geomorphic elements observed in the area are both structural and topographic 'heights' 'depressions', 'flats and 'slopes' sculptured on the topographic surface in a linear fashion. The physiography of the state shows north-south trending steep, mostly anticlinal, longitudinal (linear fashion) parallel to sub-parallel hill ranges and synclinal narrow valleys with series of parallel hammocks on topographic highs. In general, the western limbs of the anticlines are steeper than the eastern limbs. In many cases faulting has produce steep fault scarps.

Geology

T.H.D. La-Touche was the first geologist who explored the Mizo Hills. He took short traverses of the Mizo Hills falling within the then Assam-Arakan geological province. In his findings published in the records of the Geological Survey of India in 1891, the area was reported to consist of a great flysch facies of rocks comprising monotonous sequences of shale and sandstone which were thrown into north-south trending folds. He believed that the rocks were the southerly continuation of those of the Cachar Hills and were probably laid down in a delta or estuary of a large river during the late Tertiary period. Two main lithostratigraphic groups were established, viz., the Barail and the Surma. Rocks of the Tipan group are also present. All these rocks are of Tertiary age. In 1964, M.M Munshi ampped the rocks of the central part of northern Mizoram. He divided the rocks of the Surma series into Bhuban and Boko Bil stages. According to him the rocks were thrown into folds representing a series of longitudinal anticlinal effect.

Further studies in 1972 have led to sub-division of Bhuban

and Boka Bil group into lower, middle and upper formations. Different structural patterns of Barails and Surmas were studied. The rocks belonging to Surma group have been laid down in relatively shallow water, near the shore basin under conditions as would have prevailed in lacustrine or deltaic environment.

Later studies indicate that the sedimentation took place in deep sea flysch environment by the action of turbidity current mechanism.

Straitigraphy

Of the two main lithostratigraphic groups found in Mizoram, the Barail group is of Oligocence age and has a total thickness of 4,500 m. It is further subdivided into three formations, Rengi (uppermost), Jenam and Laison (lowermost). The Surma group is of Miocene age and has a total thickness of 6,000 m. It is subdivided into two formations, the upper one being Boka Bil and the lower one being Bhuban. The Surma group overlies the Brazil group with a clearly defined unconformity.

Barail Group

This group of rocks which is in the east is different from those of the Bhuban formations lying to the west. The Barials are predominantly shales and siltones with bands of weathered, medium grained yellowish sandstones. These are rather soft and micacous. Some hard and dark grey compact quartzwacke bands are present. These rocks exhibit, on weathering, pink, violet, greenish grey and white colorations.

Surma Group

The lower Bhuban formation under this group contains fine grained, compact, bluish ash and grayish coloured massive sandstones. Siltstones and silty shales also occurs. The middle Bhuban comprises compact, medium to fine grained and grey to dull yellow coloured bedded sandstones. This occurs with well laminated, iron stained, green shales, silty shales and silt with shales and muds. The upper Bhuban comprise mostly hard, compacts, massive, bluish grey to grey coloured sandstones with siltstones and shale interlamination. The shales are olive green in colour. Sandstone bands sometimes contain large calcareous boulders of various shapes and size.

The rock samples near Sairang have yielded some microfossils. These have been identified as Ostracoda: *Leguminocytheries sp., Foraminifera : Ammonia cf. beccari, Ammonia cf. pappaliloss, Globigerina sp. 1, Globigerina sp.2.*

The rocks belonging to the Boka Bil formation occur conformably over the upper Bhuban. It is represented by soft, grey coloured and medium to fine grained feldspathic sandstones. Sandy shales with interlaminated siltstones and grey sandstones also occur/ Brownish yellow ferruginous sandstones are occasionally present.

Geological Structure

The rocks of the state lie on highly compressed asymmetrical anticlinal ridges and narrow valleys with parallel to sub-parallel sub-vertical axial planes. The axes of the folds show convergence pattern in the directions of plunge. The limbs of the major folds are folded into small anticlines and synclines mostly in chevron style. The folds are long ones with axes running in nearly north-south direction, in continuation of the north Cachar Hills. The overall fold geometry maintains similarity throughout the state. The intensity of fold movements is greater in the steepy, and are possibly overturned at places.

Primary sedimentary structures recorded in the area are of deep sea flysch type structures, viz., graded bedding, flute casts, load casts, ridge structures, chevron marks, parting lineation, groove marks, ripple drift cross laminations, ripple through convolutions and complete sequence of turbidite structures. The palaeocurrent directions shown by all primary features reveal a mean southerly transport direction indicating a southerly basinal plunge.

Geological History

The rocks of the Mizo Hills are the southern extension of those of the Surma valley. They fall within the part of Tripura-Mizoram miogeosynclinal basin which evolved after the regional uplift of the Barail group of sediments from the Indian Ocean. The deposition of later sediments took place after the uplift of the Barails in a tectonic through having a 'bell-shaped' pattern.

The sediments was transported along the canyons and canyon-extension valleys to the lower slopes or continental rise, where the deposition took place from turbidity current. The thick bedded greywackes were deposited in the channel areas. The silt and shale inter-laminations were deposited in the inter-channel area. A shallow sea might have existed here during the late Boka Bil time as is evidenced by the presence of large scale planer cross-bedding, through cross-bedding and coarse grained sandstone with less clay in the top of the synclinal cores.

The Mizo Hills are south-ward continuation of the Patkai range. Geological evidence indicates that these areas formerly were a part of the estuary or delta of a large river issuing from the Himalayas in the Tertiary period. Primary evidences of such theory include marine fossils of the Tertiary age found in Mizoram. Some such fossils have been unearthen in Lunglei District. These were found embedded in grey sandstones and shales.

The beds of the Mizo Hills appear to have been laid down in a sea which was separated from the Burmese Sea during the Cretaceous times.

Mineral Resources

No major mineral deposits of economic importance have been reported so far in the state. All attempts by the Geological Survey of India were unsuccessful in locating any promising mineral occurrence of economic importance. Further exploratory operations are in progress with the objective of locating promising mineral deposits including oil and gas. Some occurrences have been reported. An occurrence of 3 m long and 10 cm thick grey pyrite bearing lignite streak in ferruginous brownish yellow soft Boka Bil sandstone has been found at a place south of Chubel village (92°25′55″: 24°03′30″). Rare disseminations of pyrite in siltstone has been found on the west bank of the Dhaleswari river between Baichhali bridge (92°39′45″ 23°50′30″) and Lengpui (92°38′45″:23°49′45″) along the road. Search in the nearby areas did not reveal more exposures of these minerals.

Building Material

The massive and hard lower and upper Bhuban sandstones are being as road metal in different parts of Mizoram. These materials is very extensively available in the state. These can be conveniently used for construction of building.

Gas and Oil

In 1964 M.M Munshi reported indications of the occurrences of oil, saline springs and a few gas seepages in the central part of northern Mizoram. Oil and Natural Gas Commission (ONGC) is working in the area and has succeeded in locating several gas seepages.

Limestone

At a place north-west of Saitual village (92°39′00″: 23°41′15″) in the Tamdil Lui nala section (92°51′30″: 23°44′30″) sporadic occurrences of small quantities of limestone have been reported.

APPENDIX - C-1

MANIFESTO TO THE INHABITANTS OF THE LUSHAI HILLS CONCERNING THE DECISION OF THE CHIEFS OF THE LUSHAI HILLS TO OFFER TOTAL RESISTANCE TO ANY INVADER

The decision of the Lushai Chiefs of the North on April 4th, and those of the South on April 16th, to offer total resistance to any invader places the Lushai Hills on the same basis of Total Defence as the peoples of England, Scotland and Wales. We are all from now on men and women, bound indissolubly together to respond to any call that may be made upon us.

Life for us from now on is no longer individual; it is communal. The failure of one village or another may bring death to many others.

We must not fail.

The road will be hard-not spectacular. We may lose life, limbs, or our loved ones. The enemy may not even come to the Lushai Hills, but we must assume he will and be prepared so we shall be strong.

It may be of interest to consider how this trial has been placed upon us.

The Chiefs of the Lushai Hills had two courses open to them:-

1. Not to oppose any invader, condoning his incursion, and falling to his promises, so broken elsewhere.

2. To oppose any invader.

How could the Chiefs follow course 1? The enemy come with no good intention. They have no peace to bring who have murdered the people of China for nearly five years. Any who have fallen to their promises are now paying the price and for the hope of physical security have now to behave as slaves, pay high taxes, and to suffer to make great the War Lords of Japan.

The Chiefs and people of Lushai could only follow course 2. But if we are to face toil and tribulation, it behoves us well to ponder. It behoves us to weigh the results that hang upon our sacrifices.

You will remember that in 1935 the British peoples enacted and Act which had for its purpose the inauguration of Dominion Status for India. The British peoples could have included the destiny of Lushai straight away with that of the Indian peoples. But they made Lushai what is now known as an "Excluded Area" and they retained the right to protect Lushai from subjection to any other majority control.

Was that not an Act which gave proof that the British people's wish was to protect Lushai Land, and to ensure that the destiny of Lushai passes to no other hands without the consent of the Lushai peoples?

Forty-five years of close contact between the Lushai and the British people have served to disclose that there is no basic incompatibility between the British and the Lushai day to day outlook on life. The same harmony cannot be claimed in relation to any close contacts elsewhere.

If Lushai Land were handed over to India or Burma what chance would we, who are Lushais, have of entering into the social and cultural framework of either power at this late stage, bearing in mind the fact that geographically or culturally we never have been a part of either.

So Lushai's destiny has really hung in the balance ever since 1935 when it became apparent that the desire of the British Government was to place the destiny of India in the hands of her own people.

If we can understand that, then how could the Chiefs and the peoples of the Lushai Hills on reflection choose any other course but to resist the invader? To remain passive at a time of trial for the peace-loving peoples of British , America, China, Russia, and all the Democracies would surely result in these great Nations ceasing, after the war, to evince any further interest in the peoples and the Land of Lushai, linking them up for ever elsewhere.

No! the Chiefs have made a wise decision. Let all of us be careful to see that we are worthy of the wisdom displayed by the Chiefs. Besides, the Lushai people have always been very loyal to His Majesty and it is natural that they should choose to stand by the Government in any hour of trial.

We penalty for any failure on our side may be cruelty and death at the hands of the enemy.

Some may feel we are not strong enough to resist. If we are too weak hearted to resist we must not expect to stand favourably in the eyes of the United Nations.

But we are strong. Let me give you some good reasons, apart from the fact that our General will do all he can to see we get what fighting help is possible.

In 1963 following upon the 1935 Government of India Act, Lushai's fate was clearly in the balance.

If we were to be deserving of the consideration of the great British peoples who have been Lushai's firmest friends for long we had to show we were a virile people, united, and keen to raise ourselves, to rise to national and united status.

The Superintendent, Lushai Hills, created certain avenues by which the Lushai peoples could prove themselves worthy. The Village Welfare Committee System was a great encouragement to a much needed unity. It brought Christians and non-Christians nearer, lessened the gap between Chiefs and people, the Chiefs and the Church, the men and the women. The 10-point code created a means for unity in our senses of what was expected to any good Lushai citizen. The Lushai Hills Cottage Industries created the means by which the skill of Lushai might spread far and wide and by which Lushai might unite together in pride and satisfaction for the gifts of skill handed down from our forefathers. Lushais themselves write from Cairo and from Quetta and from elsewhere, proud to see Lushai products being used by the Army institutions and others, while even now Lushai articles have been specially sent by the Government of India to Johannesburg, the city of Gold, in Africa, as an example of our ancient and contemporary art.

Then in 1938, you, who keep in touch with world affairs, will remember the Munich agreement of 1938, by which Mr. Chamberlain managed to put off war with Germany for one more precious year. The Superintendent, Lushai Hills, then intensified the above avenues to create our national strength and unity and intensified Circle Conferences among Chiefs, culminating in October, 1941 in a full District Durbar of Circle Representative Chiefs from the North and the South Lushai Hills. Such a body is the initial personification of Lushai national life. It would be difficult to aspire to nationhood without such institutions as the above.

Thus from disunity we have progressed to unity. From suspicion and fear and petty disputes and rivalries we have come nearer and more unified in outlook, more alive to the importance of ourselves being worthy to beseech British never to abandon us to any other power except with our consent. This happy attainment has been due very greatly to our friends the Missionaries in our midst who have spent much and their energies that we shall prosper and rise.

So if we must suffer because a grabbing enemy is not far from our and we know we struggle for something worth while, viz., the security of our whole future.

I appeal to each member of the Educational salaried cadre exert his influence among the people to obey and to help their Chiefs and village elders in their responsible tasks.

I make a personal appeal to each important member of the Lushai Church, North and South, to afford similar support to the endeavour of our unhappy peoples in meeting this threat of unprovoked aggression.

Together we can most certainly stand:

Disunited we must not only fall, but we shall bring death and destruction on ourselves far in excess of what which we may have to meet as a brave and united nation.

It is the wish of the Government that those non-Lushai who are not essential as part of the administrative war machine should leave the Lushai Hills for this short period of distress, which we hope may not be longer than one year at the most.

It is for this reason that those non-Lushais who are not directly concerned with the administration will be leaving the Hills temporarily.

The enemy is not here. The enemy may never dare to come. What we will be doing from time to time will be done so that if he comes, we shall not be taken by surprise and unprepared.

Let there be no panic. Panic is weakness, not a sign of bravery. It wastes energy, and hinders our security.

The Lushais are a manly and a martial race.

Let us never forget this truth.

APPENDIX - C-2

PROCEEDINGS OF MEETING OF THE ACCREDITED LEADERS LUSHAI HILLS HELD AT AIJAL ON 14TH AUGUST, 1947.

Chairman : Mr L.L. Peters, Superintendent, Lushai Hills (Elected)

PRESENT :

1. KHAWTINKHUMA	2. R. THANHLIRA, B.A
3. VANTHUAMA	4. PASTOR CHHUAHKHAMA
5. BRIG KAWLKHUMA,(SA)	6. KHUMA
7. LALBUAIA	8. HRANGAIA
9. MUKA	10. ROSIAMA
11. VANCHUANGA	12. CHAWNGHNUAIA
13. PHILLIPA	14 CAPT NGURLIANA (SA)
15. PACHHUNGA	16. VANLAWMA
17 VANKHUMA	18. LAIHNUNA
19. CHHUNRUMA	20. PASTOR ZAIREMA, B.Sc., B.D.
21. RINA	22. ZAWLA
23. SENA	24 ROSEMA
25 LALUPA	26. LALHEMA
27. SAIAITHANGA	28. PASTOR LIANGKHAIA
29. LALBIAKTHANGA	30. LALROPUIA
31. SUAKA	32. HMINGLIANA
33. LALANA	34. LIANHNUNA
35. PASENA	36. LIANSAILOVA, CHIEF
37. LALBUANGA, CHIEF	38. LIANZUALA, CHIEF
39. LAMHLIRA, CHIEF	40. KAMLOVA
41. CH. NGURA	42. ZAMI (MRS KHAWTINKHUMA)
43. KAPTHLUAII	44. BIAKVEKLI (MRS BUCHHAWNA)
45. LALRONGENGA	46. THANSEIA (Ex-Sub)
47. R. ZUALA (Ex-Jamadar)	48. DAHRAWKA, V.A.S
49. KAPTHIANGA	50. SAIHLIRA, B.A.

1. Resolved that owing to the unexpected acceleration of the date of transfer of power by the British Government and as the Lushais have not as yet been definitely informed

in the details as to what is to be the proposed future constitution and form of administration of the district and as section (7) sub-Section (2) of the Indian Independence Bill does not clarify the situation, it is accordingly thought that His Excellency the Governor of Assam should kindly inform them in writing as to what these are to be, also whether Lushais are at this stage allowed the option of joining any other dominion, i.e. Pakistan or Burma. Resolved further that superintendent, Lushai Hills, should kindly communicate above request of the Lushai to the Adviser to His Excellency, the Government of Assam in order to clarify these points.

2 Resolved that if the Lushais are to enter Indian Union their main demands are : -

(i) that the existing safeguards of their Customary Laws and land tenure, etc, should be remained.

(ii) that Chin Hills Regulation, 1896 and Bengal Eastern Frontier Regulation, 1873 should be retained until such time as the Lushais themselves through their District Council or other District authority declared that this can be abrogated.

(iii) that the Lushais will be allowed to opt out of the Indian Union, when they wish to do so subject to a minimum period of ten years.

Sd/- L.L PETERS
14-8-1947

Superintendent,
Lushai Hills

No. 6927-76 G of 21-8-47

Copy forwarded to all the leaders who took part in the proceedings.

Sd/- L.L PETERS

Superintendent,
Lushai Hills

APPENDIX - C-3

MEMORANDUM SUBMITTED TO HIS MAJESTY'S GOVERNMENT, GOVERNMET OF INDIA AND ITS CONSTITUENT ASSEMMBLY THROUGH THE ADVISORY SUB-COMMITTEE BY THE MIZO UNION

MIZO MEMORANDUM:

Memorandum of the case of the Mizo people for the right of territorial unity and solidarity and self-determination within the province of Assam in free India submitted to His Majesty's Government and the Government of India and its Constituent Assembly through the Advisory Sub-Committee for Assam and fully excluded areas and partially excluded areas.

Pursuant to the resolution passed by the General Assembly of the Mizo Union at Aijal in September 1946 subsequently supported by the Mizo Conference at Lakhipur (Cachar) in November 1946 this memorandum prepared by the Mizo Union and supported by the Mizos outside the Lushai Hills-Manipur State, Cachar, Tripura and the Chittagong Hill Tracts, etc.

The memorandum seeks to represent the case of Mizo people for territorial unity and integrity of the whole Mizo population and full self-determination within the province of Assam for the realization of which an appeal is made to His Majesty's Government, the Government of India and its Constituent Assembly to make a special financial provision from year to year for a period of ten years or until such time as the Mizos shall assert that they and maintain their self-determination without this financial provision.

THE PEOPLE AND THE LAND

The Mizos are a numerous family of tribes, closely knitted together by common tradition, custom, culture, mode of living, language and rites. They are spread over a wider area extending far beyond Manipur State, Cachar, Tripura State, Chittagong Hill Tracts and Burma contiguous with the boundaries of the present Lushai Hills District which was carved out arbitrarily for administrative purposes.

The Mizo people have been known under different names. They were wrongly identified as Kudis during the time of Lord Warren Hastings when Administration of Chittagong sought help of the British against the Kuki raider and it continued to be applied to the whole group until 1871 when it was supplanted by the term Lushai as a result of the active and prominent part taken by the Lushai. Sub-tribe of Mizo race, against the British Expedition known as the First Lushai Expedition . The present Lushai Hills District was thus carved out of the Mizoram for administrative convenience and the Mizo people living within the District came to be known as Lushais while the other Mizos left out of the Lushai Hills District and annexed to the surrounding districts, continued to be known as Kuki without their consent. However, the solidarity of the Mizo people as a race and a distinst block is testified by the names of places, mountains and ranges on the Lushai Hills, Cachar, Manipur, Tripura, Chittagong Hill Tracts, Burma, known and called after the name of them. Shakespeare, Stevenson, Liangkhaia, Shaw, Kingdonward and Kim of the Statesman are some of the authorities on this.

The Mizos have nothing in common with the plants nor with the Naga or Manipuri. etc. They are a distinct block. The areas now under their occupation are mostly hilly except the eastern portion of Cachar district extending to the Barial range in the North Cachar Hills.Whenever they go and wherever they are, they carry with them primitive customes, culture and mode of living in its purest origin, always calling and identifying themselves as Mizo.

The nomenclature of the word 'KUKI' was and is ever known to the Mizos; it was a name merely given to them by the neighbouring foreigners.

Again, it was wrong that the word Lushai should be used as covering all the Mizo tribes since it is misrendering of the Lusei, only sub-tribe of the Mizo race. Hence though, perhaps, not originally intended, it has created a division. Only the word 'Mizo' stands for the whole group of them all: Ludei, Hmar,Ralte,Paite,Zo, Darlawng, Kawm, Pawi, Thado, Chiru, Aimoul, Khawl, Tarau, Anal, Puram Tikhup, Vaiphei, Lakher, Langrawng, Chawrai, Bawng, Baite, Mualthuam, Kaihpen, Pangkhua, Tlanglau, Hraangkhawl, Bawmzo, Mirta, Dawn, Kumi, Khiangte, Khiang, Pangte, Khawlhring, Chawngthu, Vanchiau, Chawhte, Ngente, Rnthlei, Hnamte, Tlau, Pautu, Pawite, Vangchhia, Zawngte Fanai etc. all closely related to one another culturally, socially, economically and physically thus forming a distinct ethnical units.

TRADITIONAL ORIGIN

(a) The Mizo people in the Lushai Hills alone number 1,46,900 with an area of 8,143 square miles according to the census of 1941.

(b) The Mizo population of Manipur State contiguous to the Lushai Hills again comes to about 70,000 with and area of about 35,00 square miles.

(c) The Mizo in the Cachar District contiguous to the Lushai Hills number about 9,000 with an area of about 300 square miles.

(d) In Tripura State contiguous to the Lushai Hills, the Mizo again number approximately 7,000 with an area of about 250 square miles.

(e) In the Chittagong Hill Tracts, contiguous to the Lushai Hills, the Mizo population is generally approximated to be 15000 with an area of about 3000 square miles.

(f) In the Chin Hills (Burma) also contiguous to the Lushai Hills who are now commonly known and termed as the Chins, number not less than 90,000 with an area of about 3800 square miles occupied by them.

The total Mizo population of the contiguous area alone thus comes roughly 3,38,400 and the areas about 18,9993 square miles.

It is a great injustice that the Mizos having one and the same culture, speaking one and the same language, professing one and the same religion, and knit together by common customs and traditions should have been called and known by different names sand thrown among different people with their homeland sliced out and given to others.

The whole contiguous area of the Mizo population as detailed above occupies the middle and the most important portion of India's Eastern Frontiers. It is, therefore, the more imperative that His Majesty's Government, the Government of India and its constituent Assembly should dothe just and proper thing and grant the Mizos their just demand for TERRITORIAL UNITY AND SOLIDARITY.

MIZO HISTORY AND BRITISH CONNECTION

The Mizo people were independent, each village forming an independent unit, and their country was never subjugated by the Maharajas of Manipur, Tripura and Chittagong nor by the Kacharis. However, there had been frontier clashes between the Mizos and the neighbouring people which ultimately brought the British to the scene in 1871. The Mizo country was subsequently annexed to the British territory in 1890, when a little less than half the country was carved out for the Mizo people and name Lushai Hills while the rest have been parceled out to the adjoining districts. Since then Mizos have remained loyal, friendly and peaceful. At all time, whenever the British needed help as World War I, Abor Expedition, Houkip Rebellion, and World War II, the willing services of the Mizo people were readily available.

The Mizos have an efficient systems of administration and discipline. Being a distinct block they retain to a considerable degree their ancient and traditional laws, and customs and organizations, beginning from village under the guidance of the Chief and the Elders, while young and old have their respective leaders in all walks of life.

Except the Cachar, the Mizo people are excluded from the Government of India's Act and the areas inhabited by them are kept as a special responsibility of the Governor of the province in his capacity as the Crown Representative and the Legislature have no influence whatsoever. In other words, the Mizos have never been under the Indian Government and never had any connection with the policies and politics of the various groups of Indian opinion.

Now that the British are quitting these Mizos who have never been under the Indian Government and whose ways are all different from others, cannot be thrown on a common platform with the rest of India. It is therefore, important to the highest degree that the Mizos be given self-determination in its fullest form.

THE PRESENT GENERAL CONDITIONS OF THE COUNTRY

As stated in the foregoing paragraphs, the Mizo areas are mostly excluded. The political officer is supreme in every respect. The education is mostly carried on by the Christian Missionary groups. The general communication of the country is extremely poor. The land is extremely hilly without good roads; and the people poor and simple, primitive and divided into tribes and clans. The highest education is mostly derived from outside the district; but in mass literacy the Mizo people is highest in Assam. The people are mostly intelligent and as such given equal terms they always outshine their fellow-workers of other community in the fields and at home. They are born strategist. Their greatest short-coming is lack of finance as a result of their trade and commerce and limited scope open for them. Their areas stretch from north to south parallel with the Burma border line for defence along the eastern border of India.

This being the background, it is all the more imperative that the Mizoram be given special financial provision by the

Central from year to year while allowing them their territorial integrity as anything short of this will be detrimental to their upbringing. In other words, the Centre shall grant financial provision from year to year for the purpose of development of the country while the district shall join autonomous Assam through legislature with adequate representation and be also eligible to the provincial services with due reservations at the same time retaining their territorial integrity and self-determination: as otherwise thrown among forty crores of Indians the 3,38,400 Mizos with their unique systems of life will be wiped out of existence.

OUR CASE

In the light of the facts stated in the foregoing paragraphs and in view of geographical position and the strategical importance of the Mizoram for the defence of India and taking into consideration the unique characteristics of Mizo polity and compact block of Mizoram - this Memorandum is placed with the authority for -

1. Territorial unity and solidarity of the whole Mizo population to be known henceforth as Mizo and Mizoram for Lushai and Lushai Hills District, retaining the sole propriety fight over the land.

2. Full self-determination with the province of Assam:

   (a) With the National Council having the supreme legislative authority and executive body and judiciary within the district the composition and function of which will be prescribe by rules.

   (b) Any concurrent subjects in which the district may be connected with the autonomous province of Assam or India as a whole shall be by negotiation with the national councils which will be set up according to wishes of the general public, any legislation may be applied to the district only with sanction of the national council with any modification.

(c) Special financial provision by the Centre from year to year until such time as the Mizos shall assert that they are able to maintain their territorial and self-determination without this financial provision..

ALL ABOVE ITEMS SHALL BE SUBJECT TO REVISION ACCORDING TO THE FUTURE TREND OF EVENTS TO THE EXTENT OF SECEDING AFTER TEN YEARS.

For this end it is to be understood that the democratic system of Government in its purest form shall at the very outset be introduced. Passed and approved by the Mizo Union representatives conferences at Aijal, Lushai Hills, Assam on 22nd April, 1947.

Sd/-

KHAWTINKHUMA

President

26-4-1947

Sd/- VANTHUAMA
General Secretary
The Mizo Union, Aijal
Lushai Hills
Assam

APPENDIX - D

MEMORANDUM SUBMITTED TO THE PRIME MINISTER OF INDIA BY THE MIZO NATIONAL FRONT GENERAL HEADQUARTERS, AIZAWL, MIZORAM ON THE 30TH OCTOBER 1965

This memorandum seeks to represent the case of the Mizo people for freedom and independence, for the right of territorial unity and solidarity; and for the realisation of which a fervent appeal is submitted to the Government on India.

The Mizos, from time immemorial lived in complete independence without foreign interference. Chiefs of different clans ruled over separate hills and valleys with supreme authority and their administration was much like that of the Greek City-State of the past. Their territory or any part thereof had never been conquered or subjugated by their neighbouring states. However, there had been border disputes and frontier clashes with their neighbouring people which ultimately brought the British Government to the scene in 1844. The Mizo country was subsequently brought under the British political control in February, 1890 when a little more than half of the country was arbitrarily carved out and named Lushai Hills (now Mizo District) and the rest of their land was parceled out of their hands to the adjoining people for the sole purpose of administrative convenience without obtaining their will or consent. Scattered as they are divided, the Mizo people inseparably knitted together by their strong bond of tradition, custom, culture, language, social life and religion wherever they are. The Mizo stood as a separated nation even before the advent of the British Government having a nationally distinct and separate from that of India. In a nutshell, they are a distinct nation, created, moulded and nurtured by God and Nature

When British India was given a status by promulgation of Government of India Act of 1935, the British Government, having fully realized in the distinct and separate nationality of Mizo people, decided that they should exclude from the purview of the new constitution and they were accordingly classed as an EXCLUDED AREA in terms of the Government Order, 1936. Their land was then kept under the special responsibility of the Governor-General-in-Council in his capacity of the Crown Representative ; and the legislature of the British India had no influence whatsoever.

In other words, the Mizos had never been under the Indian Government and never had any connection with politics of the various groups of Indian opinion. When India was in the threshold of Independence, the relation of the Mizos with the British Government and also with the British India were fully realised by the Indian National Congress leaders. Their top leader and spokesman Pandit Jawaharlal Nehru released a press statement on the 19th August 1946 and stated: 'the tribal areas are defined as being those along the frontier of India which are neither part off India, nor of Burma, nor of any Indian State, nor of any foreign power.' He further stated: 'The areas are subsidized and the Governor-General's relation with the inhabitants are regulated by sanads, custom or usage. In the matter of internal administration, the areas are largely left to themselves.' Expressing the view of the Indian National Congress, he continued, 'Although the tribal areas are technically under the sovereignty of His Majesty's Government, their status, when a new Constitution comes into force in India, will be different from that of Aden over which the Governor-General no longer has executive authority. Owing to their inaccessibility and their importance to India in its defence strategy, their retention as British possession is most unlikely. One view is that with the end of sovereignty in India, the new Government of India (i.e. Independent Government of India) will enter into the same relations with the tribal areas as the Governor-General maintains now, unless the people of these areas choose to seek integration with India.'

From the foregoing statement made by Pandit Jawaharlal Nehru and the Government of India Act of 1935, it is quite clear that the British Government left the Mizo Nation free and independent with the right to decide their future political destiny.

Due solely to their political immaturity, ignorance and lack of consciousness of their fate, representatives of the Mizo Union, the largest political organization at that time and Fifty accredited Mizo leaders representing all political organizations including representatives of religious denominations and social organizations that were in existence submitted their demand and choose integration with free India imposing condition, inter alia. "THAT THE LUSHAIS WILL BE ALLOWED TO OPT OUT OF INDIAN UNION WHEN THEY WISE TO DO SO SUBJECT TO A MINIMUM PERIOD OF TEN YEARS."

The political immaturity and ignorance which lead the Mizo people to the misguided choice of integration with India was a direct result of the banning by the British Government of any kind of political organization till April 1946 within Mizoland which was declared 'a political area.'

During the fifteen years of close contact and association with India, the Mizo people had not been able to feel that their joys and sorrows have really ever been shared by India. They do not, therefore, feel Indian. Being created a separate nation they cannot go against the nature to cross the barriers of nationality. They refused to occupy a place within India as they consider it to be unworthy of their prosperity. Nationalism and patriotism inspired by the political consciousness has now reached its maturity and the cry for political self-determination is the only wish and inspiration of the people, ne plus ultra, the only final and perfect embodiment of social living for them. The only aspiration and political cry is the creation of MIZORAM, a free and sovereign state to govern herself, to work out her own destiny and to formulate her own foreign policy.

To them Independence is not even a problem or subject of controversy: there cannot be dispute over the subject nor could there be any different of opinion in the matter. It is only a recognition of human rights and to let others live in the dignity of human person.

While the present world is strongly committed to freedom and self-determination of all nations, large or small, and to promotion of Fundamental Human Rights, and while the Indian leaders are strongly wedded to that principle - taking initiative for and championing the cause of Afro-Asian countries, even before the World body, particularly deploring domination and colonization of the weaker nations by the stronger, old and new, and advocating peaceful co-existence, settlement of international disputes of kind through the medium of non-violence and in condemning weapons mankind, the Mizo people firmly believed that the Government of India and their leaders will remain true to their policy and that they shall take into practice what they advocate, blessing the Mizo people with their aspiration for freedom and independence per principle that no one is good enough to govern another man without that man's consent.

Though known as head-hunters and a martial race, the Mizos commit themselves to a policy of non-violence in their struggle and have no intention of employing any other means to achieve their political demand. If, on the other hand, the Government of India brings exploitative and suppressive measures into operation, employing military might against the Mizo people as id done in the case of Nagas, which God forbid, it would be equally erroneous and futile for both the parties for a soul cannot be destroyed by weapons.

For this end, it is in goodwill and understanding that the Mizo Nation voices her rightful and legitimate claim of full self-determination through this memorandum. The Government of India, in their turn and in conformity with the unchangeable truth expressed and resolved among the text of HUMAN RIGHTS by the United Nations in its august assembly that in order to maintain peace and tranquility among mankind every nation, large or small, may of right be free to work out her own destiny, to formulate her own internal and external policies and shall accept and recognize her political independence. Would it not be a selfish motive and design of India, and would it not amount to an act of offence against humanity if the Government of India claim Mizoram as part their territory and try to retain her as their possession against the national will of the Mizo people simple because their land is important for India's defence strategy ?

Wheather the Mizo Nation should shed her tears in joy to establish firm and lasting friendship with India in war in peace or sorrow and anger, is upto the Government of India to decide.

Sd/- S. LIANZUALA
General Secretary,
Mizo National Front, Mizoram.

Sd/- LALDENGA
President
Mizo National Front,
Mizoram

Dated Aizawl the 30th October 1965

APPENDIX - E

1. MEMORANDUM OF SETTLEMENT PREAMBLE

2. RESTORATION OF NORMALCY

3. **LEGAL ADMINISTRATIVE AND OTHER STEPS**

(See Pages 176-178)

APPENDIX - F

Ministry of External Affairs (BSM DIVISION)

INDIA-BANGLADESH RELATIONS

General

1. India's relations with Bangladesh are cordial, friend and cooperative and wide-ranging. Cultural affinities with India in general and West Bengal in particular and ethnic linkages with India's north-eastern States greatly enhance the level of people-to-people contacts.

Visits

2. India and Bangladesh interact regularly on various operational matters. There has also been a regular flow of high level visits. The last VVIP visits took place in June 1999 when Prime Minister Shri Atal Bihari Vajpayee accompanied by a high-level official delegation including the External Affairs Minister; Shri Jaswant Singh visited Dhaka on the occasion of the inaugural u\run of the bus from Calcutta to Dhaka. Shri Brajesh Mishra, Principal Secretary to PM and National Security Adviser visited Dhaka on October 26-27,2001 as Special Envoy following formation of the new Government in Bangladesh.

3. Begum Khaleda Zia, Prime Minister of Bangladesh called on PM on January 4, 2002 at Kathmandu on the sidelines of the SAARC Summit. The Prime Minister of Bangladesh met PM at Islamabad during the SAARC summit in January 2004. Various regional and bilateral issues were discussed during the meeting.

4. Mr. M. Morshed Khan, Foreign Minister of Bangladesh paid an official visit to India on 16-17 June 2002 and again on 13-16, February, 2003. He again visited India from 31 May

- 4 June 2004 as a special envoy of the Prime Minister of Bangladesh after the formation of the government carrying a letter from the Prime Minister of Bangladesh addressed to the Prime Minister of India and to Smt. Sonia Gandhi. The Finance Minister of Bangladesh visited India in May 2003.

5. The External Affairs Minister Shri Yashwant Sinha paid a goodwill visit to Bangladesh on 24-25 August 2002 and again in July 2003 for the bilateral Joint Economic Commission meeting.

6. Foreign Secretary Shri Kanwal Sibal visited Dhaka from 29 –30th April, 2003 for the Foreign Secretary level consultations. Foreign Secretary Shri Shashank visited Bangladesh from 8 - 11 March 2004. During the visit decision was taken to resume the 'Trade talks" to discuss FTA between the two countries and the issue of Non Trade barriers. It was also agreed to hold Foreign Office consultations in the first half of June 2004 as also to reactivate the Home Secretary level dialogue between the two countries (Dates are being worked out)

Infrastructural links

7. Proposals for cooperation the transportation sector are under discussion between the two governments. These include passenger and freight movement by road and rail and movement of freight through IWT mode. In a recent development, Government of India has designated Jet Airway and Air Sahara as Indian carriers besides Indian Airlines and Air India to operate agreed services between India and Bangladesh. Jet Airways and Air Sahara have approached the civil aviation authorities of Bangladesh for the operationalisation of the proposed air services.

Bus services

8. An Agreement to commence a bus service between Calcutta and Dhaka was inaugurated on 19 June'99 in the presence of the Prime Minister of both countries. Talks for renewal of the Agreement / Protocol for the Calcutta –

Dhaka bus service were held on 14 –15 March 2002 and the Agreement has been further extended till October 2004.

9. During MOS(EA)'s visit to Dhaka in January 2000, it was agreed that a bus service between Agartala and Dhaka would be started. Subsequently, an Agreement and a Protocol regarding operation of the proposed bus service were signed in Dhaka in July 2001. The bus service started in September,2003.

Rail links

10. There are three broad gauge (BG) rail links : (i) Gede (India)-Darsana (BD),(ii) Singhabad-Rohanpuur (BD) and (iii) Petrapole (India) Benapole(BD). Wagons are taken to and from the border by the engines of each side. Two metre gauge links exist between Birol-Radhikapur and Shahbazpur-Mohishashonpur. A working agreement was signed in July 2000 to restore the Petrapole - Bebapole railway link. The freight train, which was formally inaugurated in January 2001. It is expected to considerably facilitate movement of cargo trade takes place. An agreement between the Government of India and the Government of Bangladesh for Running of Passenger Train Services between India and Bangladesh was also signed in July 2001 in Dhaka. Regular service is yet to commence.

11. Both sides have also agreed on the need to link Agartala and Akhaura by rail.

Inland Water Transit & Trade [IWT&T] Protocol

12. The IWT&T Protocol has been operational since 1972 and is renewable every two years. It permits the movement of goods and barges/vessels through the river systems of Bangladesh on eight specific routes between Calcutta and points in Assam (Dhubri, Karimganj). Talks were held in Dhaka in October, 1999 where the Protocol on Inland Water Transit and Trade between India and Bangladesh and India was renewed for two years upto October 2001. Pending the holding of the Protocol renewal talks the IWTT Protocol has

been extended till 3rd August 2004. Under the Protocol, Calcutta, Haldia, Pandu and Karimganj on the Indian side and Narayanganj, Sirajganj, Khulana and Mongla on the Bangladesh side have been declared as Ports of Call. However, there is no provision for mutimodal transhipment of Indian goods through Bangladesh.

Trade & Economic Ties

Trade

13. India's exports to Bangladesh showed a significant increase in the early 90s. There was a decline in 1996-97 and 1997-98 in our exports to Bangladesh due to fall in rice exports. The exports rose again in 1998 -99 due to large-scale import of rice by Bangladesh due to the devastating floods of 1998. Bangladesh exports to India have been growing since 1197-98. Recent trade figures are as follows:

(In US$ Million)

	1990-00	*2000-01*	*2001-02*	*2002-03*
Exports to BD	932.58	1184.00	940.00	1250.00
Imports from BD	64.88	62.28	50.50	84.00
Trade Gap	867.70	1121.72	889.60	1166.00

14. Major items of export from India are : foodgrains (this is sporadic, dependent on floods and can be very substantial as in 1990-91 and 1998-99 (US$ 267 million and US$ 526 million respectively), cotton yarn, fabrics, made-ups, machinery, instruments, glass/glassware, ceramics and coal. Major items of import from Bangladesh are: raw jute, jamdani saris, inorganic chemicals, leather etc.

Tariff Concessions to Bangladesh

15. India has been progressively reducing tariffs for Bangladesh items under the Bangkok Agreement and under SAPTA. India has extended tariff concessions to Bangladesh on more than 2000 tariff lines under SAPTA. All Quantitative

Restrictions have been removed in full for SAARC country imports from 1st August 1998.

16 Bangladesh has been requesting for unilateral tariff concessions on select items of export interest to Bangladesh to help them reduce trade deficit with India. During PM's visit to Bangladesh in 1999, he had announced India's acceptance. In principle, of the request for duty-free access on a non-reciprocal basis for select items of export interest to Bangladesh. While indicating this, he added that a Joint Group of Experts should meet to discuss this issue along with that of restoration of multi-modal communication links between the two countries and framework for border trade.

17. However, as a gesture of goodwill, India had offered 100% tariff concessions on 16 products groups consisting of 40 tariff lines to Bangladesh during the Trade Review Talks in April 2002 held in Dhaka. Duty free access was announced for items under another 39 tariff lines during the Trade Review Talks held in March 2003.

Trans-shipment

18. During the visit of the Commerce Minister of Bangladesh in May 1999, it was agreed to set up a Joint Group of Experts of examine modalities for (a) the movement of goods from one point in India to another through Bangladesh by Bangladesh carriers, (b) border trade and (c) tariff concessions. Meeting of the Joint Group of Experts is yet to be held.

Credit

19. An Agreement to extend a credit line of Rs.200 crore to Bangladesh was signed in June '99. the Bangladesh Government has allocated the amount of Rs. 200 crores for import of double-decker buses by BRTC (Rs. 30 crores), import of 13 BG locomotives by BD Railways (Rs. 92 crores) and import of rail, sleepers, fastenings, etc. for dual guage in Dhaka-Yoydevpur section of BD Railways (Rs. 78 crores).The credit line has been almost fully utilised. Currently

discussions are on for extension of a $150 million dollar denominated credit line to Bangladesh.

Investment

20. There are 28 Indian joint ventures in Bangladesh with equity participation equivalent to US $ 16.5923 million and 7 wholly owned subsidiaries with total equity of US $0.6136 million (as on October 30, 2000). Areas covered include textile spinning, building industry, chemicals, software data processing, and automobiles sector etc.

Joint Economic Commission

21. The External Affairs Minister visited Dhaka in July 2003 as co-chairperson to attend the 6th meeting of the Joint Economic Commission between India and Bangladesh. All issues of economic and commercial interest were discussed in a comprehensive manner. Discussions were held on a possible new line of credit that could be denominated in US dollars. A number of proposals in the Railway sector were discussed including those on introduction of containerised services by rail and the Sealdah-Joydevpur passenger rail link. It was agreed that the Joint Working Group at the level of Joint Secretaries of Commerce would meet in Dhaka by the middle of October 2003 to begin negotiations on a bilateral Free Trade Agreement. A decision was taken to flag off the Dhaka-Agartala Bus service. Cooperation in new areas such as S&T. IT and Agriculture was also discussed. It was agreed that the Standing Committee of officials would meet once when the JEC convenes and once in between the sessions of the JEC to effectively monitor developments.

Trade Agreement

22. The Trade Agreement between India and Bangladesh was signed on 4 October 1980. The Agreement had been since then extended for 3 years with mutual consent. On its last expiry, Bangladesh suggested that the Agreement be reviewed fully; hence its validity has been extended pending a thorough reassessment. The Trade Agreement provides for the holding

of regular trade review talks. The Bangladesh Commerce Secretary visited New Delhi on May 10-11, 2000 for Trade Review Talks in March, 2003 in New Delhi.

Regional Organisations

23. India and Bangladesh are both founder members of SAARC and BIMST-EC, the new grouping established in 1997 for cooperation around the Bay of Bengal. The main sectors of co-operation in BIMST-EC are trade, investment, industrial cooperation, human resources development, tourism, energy, transportation, infrastructure, technology, fisheries, agriculture and nature resources.

Sharing of Water of Common Rivers

Treaty on sharing of Ganga Waters

24. The Treaty between India and Bangladesh on sharing of the Ganga Waters at Farakka was signed on 12 December 1996. Sharing of waters of the Ganga under the Treaty is based in an indicative formula viz., when the total available water is 70,000 cusecs or less, each side receives 50%; when the total flow is 70,000-75,000 cusecs, Bangladesh gets 35,000 with the balance for India; when the total flow is 75,000 cusecs or more, India will take 40,000 cusecs and release the balance for Bangladesh.

25. The sharing formula is subject to the provision that during the driest part of the lean season (i.e., March 1 to May 10) India and Bangladesh will each received a guaranteed 35,000 cusecs of water in 3 alternate 10-day periods each. There is an emergency provision for consultations in case the total amount of water available falls below 50,000 cusecs. The Treaty is for 30 years, with a provision for reviews after every five years. Either side can also call for a review after 2 years.

26. The Treaty has worked well during the last six lean seasons; the sharing arrangements are due for review.

Joint Rivers Commission (JRC)

27. During that visit of the Prime Minister to Dhaka in January 1997, it was decided to reactivate the Joint Rivers Commission (JRC) at the level of Water Resources Ministers. In July 1997, our Water Resource Minister visited Dhaka and discussed a wide range of issues. A Joint Committee of Experts (JCE) headed by Secretary, Water Resources was set up in 1997, to hold discussions on sharing of waters of common rivers. Priority was accorded by the commission to sharing the Teesta waters. So far six meetings of the JCE have been held, the last in January 2004. Since there was a wide difference in the position of the two sides, the JCE constituted a Joint Technical group (JTG) mandated to suggest the Terms of reference for Joint Scientific Studies and Interim sharing formula for the sharing of lean season flows. One meeting of the JTG has been held in May 2004. The 34th Session of the JRC was held in Dhaka on January 12-13, 2001. Both sides discussed, inter alia, the issues of embankments on Common/border River, sharing of the Teesta waters and other common rivers, improvement of flood forecasting and warning and sharing of experiences on containing arsenic contamination of the underground water. Expert level meetings on various aspects of rivers waters have been taking place regularly. The last meeting of the JRC took place in September,2003

Border Management and Security

28. Government has shared concerns on several issues related to border management cooperation with Bangladesh, including control of smuggling, illegal immigration, trafficking in women and children and insurgency. The Government of Bangladesh has assured India of its commitment not to allow the use of its territory for activities prejudicial to Indian interests.

29 There is a system of institutionalised interaction for discussion on border management through the meeting of the Home Secretaries, Joint Working Group and the Director

General level talks between the Border Security Force and the Bangladesh Rifles. These have been taking place regularly. The Bangladesh Home Minister visited India in December 1999; the 8th Joint Working Group Meeting was held in Dhaka from January 22-23, 2003. The India-Bangladesh Home Secretary level talks took place in New Delhi on April 26-27,2000. Director General-level talks between BSF and Bangladesh Rifles have been held regularly, the recent ones in January 2004 at Delhi and from 28 April -3 May, 2004 at Dhaka.

30. Despite the institutional mechanisms for resolving border-management issues, the India-Bangladesh border witnessed serious incident in April 2001. The Bangladesh Government has been apprised at the highest level about the depth and intensity of the national feelings in India. The Government feels that the incidents reflected criminal adventurism on the part of certain elements in Bangladesh and should not be permitted to affect the traditionally close and friendly relations between the two countries. Both Governments have instructed the border forces to exercise restraint and meet regularly to deal with any problem that may arise from time to time.

Revised Visa Regime

31. Visa regime between India and Bangladesh is governed by the revised travel arrangements signed in Dhaka in May 2001. These arrangements seek to facilitate grant of long term multiple entry visas to businessmen, investors, professionals, research scholars and students and for people visiting on medical grounds.

32. There is extensive people-to-people contact between India and Bangladesh. Our Missions in Bangladesh (Dhaka, Chittagong and Rafshahi) issue some 1000 visas a day on an average or 300,000 visa a year. There is no visa fee.

33. It is estimated that well over 50,000 students from Bangladesh pursue higher studies in India; around 100 students come under various scholarship schemes, while the

majority are self-financing. Cultural troupes from India visit Bangladesh regularly under ICCR and other auspices. The Indian High Commission has set up a Dance and Music Teaching Centre in Dhaka. The last India-Bangladesh Cultural and Academic Exchange Programme (CAEP) expired on Dec. 31 1999. The CAEP will, however, remain in force till a new agreement is signed. The commercial screening of Indian films in Bangladesh is banned. The former Government of Eat Pakistan introduced the ban in mid '60s and since then it has not been revoked.

APPENDIX - G

Ministry of External Affairs
(SEA-I Division)

INDIA-MYANMAR RELATIONS

Introduction

Indo-Myanmar relations are rooted in shared cultural and religious ties. Both countries also share a long land and maritime boundary. A large population of Indian origin lives in Myanmar. Geo-strategic factors make it logical for India and Myanmar to have a close relationship.

2. Our relations with Myanmar are reflective of our common desire to cooperate with each other in order to promote peace and tranquility along the border, to achieve sustained economic development in both our countries and to foster people-to-people interaction. A Treaty of friendship was signed in 1951. Recent years have seen a steady growth of exchanges and broad-basing of ties.

Current Status of Bilateral Relations

3. Institutional mechanisms for facilitating regular dialogue on issues of bilateral interest have been set up, mainly in the form of Foreign Office Consultations (held at the level of Foreign Secretary/Deputy Foreign Minister in Yangon in 1993; New Delhi, 1994; Yangon, 1999; New Delhi, 2000; Yangon 2002, October, 2003) National Level and Sectoral Level Meetings (9th NLM was held in Yangon in October, 2003); Border Liaison Meetings (the 22nd Border Liaison Meeting was held in April, 2003).

4. An agreement on curbing demand and preventing illicit trafficking in narcotic drugs and psychotropic substances and related matters was signed during the visit of Foreign Secretary in 1993. A Tripartite Maritime Agreement among

India, Myanmar and Thailand determining the trijunction poit in the Andaman Sea was concluded in October 1993. Gen. Maung Aye's visit to Shillong in January, 2000 and the talks during it at the military to military level and at the political level with the delegation led by the Commerce Minister, Shri Murasoli Maran prepared the ground for his week long visit to India in November, 2000 at the invitation of the Vice President. Gen. Maung Aye's delegation included the Myanmar Deputy Prime Minister and seven other ministers. Gen. Maung Aye called on the President and PM, and had meetings with the Vice President, EAM, Home Minister, the leader of opposition and others. Gen. Maung Aye's visit was significant in that it led to a resumption of bilateral cooperation.

5. High-level exchanges have continued. EAM visited Myanmar in February, 2001 for the inauguration of the Tamu-Kalemyo road and the Remote Sensing and Data Processing Centre. In April, 2002 EAM again visited Yangon for the India-Myanmar-Thailand Ministerial Meeting on Transport Linkages. The Foreign Secretary visited Myanmar in November 2002 and the Myanmar Foreign Minister visited India in January, 2003. EAM and FM Win Aung signed a Protocol on Constitutions between the Ministry of External Affairs of the Republic of India and the Minister Foreign Affairs of the Union of Myanmar. Myanmar Foreign Minister U Win Aung visited once again as a Special Envoy of Sr. General Than Shwe, Chairman, SPDC from July 10-11,2003. During the visit he met EAM and called on PM to hand over a letter from Senior General Than Shwe addressed to him. U. Win Aung explained the position of the Myanmar Government on the domestic developments evolving detention of Aung San Suu Kyi on May 30, 2003. Our Minister for Commerce and Industry Shri Arun Jaitley visited Myanmar from July 14-16, 2003 to sign an MoU on the establishment of a Joint Trade Committee. Shri Arun Shourie, Minister for Communications & Information Technology visited Myanmar from August 25 - 30, 2003. A MoU on IT cooperation was signed during the visit. The Vice President visited Myanmar

from November 2 - 6, 2003 at the invitation of the Vice Chairman, SPDC Vice Senior General Maung Aye. This was the first VVIP visit from India since 1987.

Forthcoming Visits

6. There are pending invitations on our side to the President, PM, Home Minister, HRD Minister, Minister for Communications & IT and Disinvestment, and the Lt. Governor of Delhi. Pending invitations on the Myanmar side include those to Secretary-1, the Minister of National Planning & Economic Development, and the Chairman of the Civil Service Selection & Training Board. The Myanmar side had proposed a visit by Chairman, SPDC in February, 2004 but in view of domestic developments, PMO has postponed consideration of the visit to the second half of the year.

Re-opening of Consulates

7. The improvement in relations has also manifested itself in the re-opening of our Consulate General in Mandalay in July, 2002, formally inaugurated during Foreign Secretary visit in November 2002. The Myanmar Consulate General in Kolkata started functioning in September, 2002.

Economic and Commercial Cooperation

8. Projects: An important plank of our policy has been to foster cooperation with Myanmar by implementing mutually beneficial cross border projects. The upgradation of the 160 km. Long Tamu-Kalewa road in Myanmar across Manipur was taken up in 1997 and completed at a cost of about Rs. 120 crores by the Border Roads Organisation. It was inaugurated by EAM in February 2001 and, under a MoU signed in May, 2001, GOI is committed to maintaining the road for a period of six years. GOI have also offered to build the Rhi-Tiddim and Rhi-Falaam road sections across Mizoram. A technical team from India visited Myanmar for discussions on these road sections in June 2003. RITES has recently submitted a financial and technical proposal for the project which is under examination.

9. With regard to the Kaladan Multimodal Transport Project, RITES have completed the DPRs for both the IWT component and the highway component. These reports have been sent to the Myanmarese government for comments and have been sent internally to the Ministries of Commerce, Shipping, Road Transport & Highways and State Government of Mizoram for comments. A composite delegation led by JS (SEA-I) visited Myanmar in May, 2004 and held discussions with Myanmar side. It was decided to hold a Senior Officials Meeting (SOM) on the Project in Yangon in September, 2004.

10. The Myanmar side had proposed a hydro-electric project on the Chindwin River at Tamanthi across Nagaland. Data collection etc. is being carried out. A pre-feasibility study has been proposed by NHPC, which has been approved subject to certain conditions which are being met. ONGC Videsh Ltd. and GAIL have acquired 20% and 10% of participating interest in the A-1 block off the Rakhine coast. ONGCVL had also put their bid for A-III Offshore Gas Structure but the contract was offered to DAEWOO of Korea. However, with the strong efforts by our Mission, the Myanmar Ministry of Energy has now organized a tripartite Meeting for OVL and DAEWOO on 3rd August, 2004.

Credit Lines

11. In April 1998, a credit line of US $ 10 million was extended to Myanmar, which utilised for rolling stock and industrial equipment. Another credit line of US $15 million credit was provided in November, 2000 and used for import from India of power generators and transmission equipment, textile printing and dyeing machinery, bicycle parts, sewing machine parts and setting up a steel foundry. In October, 2002 Government of Myanmar requested another credit line of US $ 25 million, an agreement for which was signed during the visit of the Myanmarese Deputy Foreign Minister for Foreign Office Consultations in October, 2003. Separately, EXIM Bank of India has offered a credit line of US $5 million to the Myanmar Foreign Trade Bank(MFTB) and/or the Myanmar Investment & Commercial Bank, or to both jointly.

12. A credit line of US $10 million has also been offered for financing of four projects discussed during the visit of the Indian Minister for IT & Communications to Myanmar in August 2003 in the areas of Rural Telecom, E-learning, E-Governance and an Optical Fibre Link between Tamu and Moreh. Now, we are proposing to establish an OFC Link along the Trilateral Highway between India, Myanmar and Thailand, response on which is still awaited from Myanmar side.

13. India has also offered a Credit Line of the amount of US$ 56 million for upgradation of the Yangon-Mandalay Rail Link. The composite delegation led by JS (SEA-I) and comprising representatives from RITES, Railway Ministry and EXIM Bank sorted out the issue with Myanmar Ministry of Rail Transportation in May,2004. It was decided that out of the credit line of 56 million US dollars, 28million US dollars would be spend on purchase of railway engines and rolling stock and rest would be spent on conduct study on the exact requirement of Myanmar Railways, which would be funded by MEA.

Trade

14. India-Myanmar trade grew steadily in the 1990s to reach a level of US$328 million in 1997-98. In 2002-02 the trade turnover amounted to US$ 427.9 million. In 2001-02 Myanmar's exports to India were of the order of US$ 354.74 million. Myanmar's imports from India for the 2001-02 was US $ 82.26 million. In 2002-02, India was the second largest market for Myanmar's exports.

15. India's imports from Myanmar are dominated by agricultural and forest based products. Myanmar is the second largest supplier of beans and pulses to India, next only to Australia, accounting for one third of India's total requirements of imported pulses. Myanmar contributes to nearly one fifth of India's imports of timber, second only a Malaysia. India's exports to Myanmar; though small, range from primary commodities to manufactured products. Primary and semi-

finished steel along with steel bars and rods constitute over half of India's exports' pharmaceuticals are the next most important item. Indian drugs and pharmaceuticals have established a market presence and major Indian pharmaceutical companies like Ranbaxy and Dr. Reddy's Laboratories are represented in the country. Export of plant and machinery and consumer goods is though small, is showing potential.

16. A Joint Trade Committee has been set up at the ministerial level. The MoU for establishing this mechanism was signed during the visit of Minister of Commerce in July 2003. A target for bilateral trade of US$ 1 billion was set for the year 2006.

Border Trade

17. Although trade in traditional goods on head basis has been the practice since a long time, the Border Trade Agreement signed in 1994 and operationalised in April, 1995 gave it a legal framework. Presently, Moreh-TAMu in the Manipur sector is the sole border trade point. A second border trading point at Zowkhatar-Rhi is due to be opened shortly.

18. In October,1998 it was decided to allow trade on Letter of Credit basis and an MOU on banking arrangements for L/C trade was signed under which the Myanmar Economic Bank at Tamu and the United Bank of India at Moreh are the designated banks for negotiating L/Cs. Border trade is also permissible in cash US Dollars.

Commercial Contracts

19. There has been a welcome increase in institutional contacts between the business communities. Union of Myanmar Federation of Chambers of Commerce and Industry (UMFCCI) and CII and the Myanmar Computer Federation (MCF) in February 2001. At a luncheon meeting addressed by the Myanmar Foreign Minister in New Delhi on 20 January, 2003 CII announced a five point action plan on Myanmar

proposing inter alia, made-in India Show in Yangon in February, 2004.

Science & Technology

20. A Science and Technology Agreement signed in 1999, during the visit of Myanmar's S&T Minister to India, provides a structured format to cooperation through a Joint Working Group (JWG). The JWG held two meetings in April, 2000 and December, 2001. The third meeting was held in December, 2001. A joint oceanographic survey of the Andaman Sea was carried out in April-May 2002. ISRO assisted Myanmar in setting up of a data processing centre in Yangon for remote sensing applications and agreed to supply satellite data free of charge for two years. The Centre was inaugurated during EAM's visit to Myanmar in February, 2001.

HRD

21. HRD has emerged as an important area of bilateral cooperation. From 44 in 1995-96, 99 Myanmar candidates have already gone to India in 2002-03 out of a total 103 slots under the TCS of Colombo Plan, ITEC and the GCCS of ICCR. In addition to these schemes, training has also been imparted to Myanmar officials under different on going projects and three Myanmar students were admitted to IISc, Bangalore in 2002 for post graduate course in aerospace engineering. An MoU has been signed on the deputation of teaching personnel from India for short-term courses at universities in Myanmar (MEA-Ed.CIL-Government of Myanmar).

Culture

22. Performances by Indian cultural troupes in Myanmar have been organized on a regular basis since 1997. Along side, we have also sponsored visits of Myanmar cultural troupes of India. We have also extended assistance in imparting training to Myanmar archaeologists in India, dating of cultural artefacts, and presented books on religion, art and culture to various institutions in Myanmar. A bilateral Cultural

Cooperation Agreement was signed during the visit of the Myanmar Cultural Minister to India in January-February, 2001. In October, 2002 Department of Culture forwarded a draft Cultural Exchange Programme (CEP), for implementing the Cultural agreement on a sustained basis, which is under consideration of the Myanmar side.

23. The shared heritage of Buddhism provides an added dimension. Buddhist pilgrimage groups, sponsored by the Myanmar Government have been given gratis visas since 1996. Myanmar maintains monasteries in Bodh Gaya; these have been run from the pre-independence days.

Regional Cooperation

24. Myanmar's membership of ASEAN, BIMST-EC and Mekong Ganga Cooperation has introduced a regional/sub-regional dimension in our belateral relations with it and imparted added significance in the context of our 'Look East" policy. At ASIAN + Indian Summit in November , 2002. Myanmar supported our case for such Summit to be held on an annual basis. A few proposals for cooperation are under discussion with Myanmar within the framework of ASEAN's IAI programme.

Trilateral Highway among India, Myanmar and Thailand

25. At a trilateral ministerial level India-Myanmar-Thailand meeting held in Yangon on 5-6 April, 2002 it was agreed that the sides would cooperate on the construction of a highway from Moreh in India to Mae Sot in Thailand through Bagan in Myanmar. The sides also agreed to promote a highway from Kanchanaburi in Thailand to the Dawei port in Myanmar and from there the shipping links to Indian ports. At the last meeting of the Foreign Ministers held in New Delhi in December, 2003 the financing of phase one of the highway was considered. The outcome of the meeting was that Thailand agreed to finance upgradation of the part of the highway close to their border from Thaton to Myawaddy (198 km) through a soft loan of US$ 58.608 million.

26. India agreed to consider offer of a Line of Credit at concessional terms to the Government of Myanmar for financing new construction from Chaungma-Yinmabin (30 km) and Lingadaw-Letsegan-Pakokku (48 km.). These links would establish a serviceable road link from Moreh to Mandalay. It was also agreed to consider similar financing of the upgradation to two-lane standard of the YinmabinPale-Lingadaw (50km) road. This would provide a link between Yangon and Bagan through which the highway must fun. Further, it was agreed to consider, subject to internal approvals, financing of the upgradation of the Bagan-Meiktila (132 km.) segments. However, subsequent to the meeting the Myanmar Foreign Minister in a letter to EAM has made some proposals to the effect that Myanmar itself would construct the highway with financial assistance from Thailand and India. This matter is under examination.

2

LINGUISTIC AND CULTURAL AFFINITY OF ZO PEOPLE

Introduction

The subject as originally assigned to me was "Language and Culture Affinity of Zo People". I have taken the liberty of amending it as given above, with a view to focusing it on the direction of study I wish to pursue. There are two obvious ways to approach this topic; one is to investigate the linguistic and cultural varieties amongst the sub-groups or tribes comprised by what is collectively termed as Zo people or even nation (perhaps, this what the designers of the seminar originally intended); and the other way is to study the connection and interrelatedness between Zo group of languages/sub-cultures and other languages and cultures belonging to non-Zo peoples. I have chosen to adopt the second approach for reasons to be presently made clear. While clarifying the reasons for electing the second option, this paper will also, hopefully, throw some light on the unity or oneness of the various Zo tribes, rather than a mere "affinity of their cultures and languages".

The first and foremost reason, in the finding of the author of this paper, is that these tribes - no matter how and what they variously call themselves or are called by others: Kuki, Chin, Laimi, Paite, Thado, Sukte, Hmar, Mara, Pawi, Ralte, Vaiphei, Sukte, Lushai, Mizo, Teddim, Sizang, gangte, Darlong, Biate, Kom, Lusei, Matu, even Arakanese etc., - are sub-groups or tribes belonging to one people, who are referred to as Zos in this paper. That this is so, is most evidently manifested in the manner in which they react or respond to one another when the members of any of these groups are thrown together, particularly in places far away from their own abodes, in the midst of "outsiders", who are truly alien to their own groups, such as whom they call "vias" (plain people of India) or "kawls or kawl vais" (plain people of Myanmar) and, of course, amongst other distant and alien peoples. The sensation most poignantly felt by these people at such encounters is that of a special feeling of kinship or of an emotional bonding, exclusive of others around them. This is an acknowledged fact of near universal experience, especially among the less educated, with less frequent exposure to the world outside of their native areas. Such an awareness of a sense of community and comradeship is usually most acute when there are faced with a tragedy or under the circumstances of adversity. This is no racial consciousness, though it may be akin to it; nor is difference of languages/ dialects barrier to it. This sense of belonging to a group/ people is essentially intuitive and cannot be explained except by the concept that they must, indeed, have belonged to one proto-tribe, the name of which is now variedly interpreted by them. Perhaps, this awareness springs from a collective memory of the peoples, usually loosely referred to as "of Zo ancestry or progeny" (Zo hnahthlak).

The second reason is that it is highly doubtful if the languages spoken by what we term here as "sub-groups" of Zo can be considered languages, rather than dialects, in scientific linguistic parlance. The author is proficient in Mizo (Lusei) and Hmar, and is familiar with Lai, Paite, Thado and Vaiphei dialects and has visited and interacted with local residents in Tahan, Khampat, Falam, Tedim and Haka (Halka) in Myanmar and Saiha, Lawngtlai, Haflong, Churachandpur, Imphal and Kangpokpi in India. these places are spread out almost in the entire region in which the tribes of Zo ancestry are said to be located. The writer has had no real difficulty in elementary communication with the local people in these localities, even though he has not undergone any formal training even for one day in the dialects spoken in these places. Besides, it is a common experience that a few days' interaction with a person from a different dialect-area is sufficient to acquire a rudimentary proficiency for inter-dialect communication. The so-called Zo languages therefore appear to be only dialects, which have evolved over time from their original common language in their respective locations. And a comparative study per se of these dialects is not likely to contribute substantially to the search for Zo origin - a subject into which this paper is also intended to add a supplementary input. (It must be admitted, however, that a comparative study of the dialects will be a principal instrument for empirical substantiation of the above assumption. This will need to be undertaken separately and, at any rate, cannot be adequately done within the length of a seminar paper).

(While one is on the issue of the dialects, it may be pertinent to mention the view that what is now officially known as Mizo, derived largely from Lusei (Duhlian) dialect and most widely current in use in Mizoram, is now acquiring a status of a lingua franca among the Zo dialects, for reasons too complex and sometimes too obvious to be covered in this paper. In this case, it has apparently reached a stage where it can be called "Zo language". And this is worth a serious consideration. One thing can be said about it for certain, though, that is - if it resists assimilation into it of words and expressions from other dialects, its growth as the lingua franca will be arrested.)

Thus, as already indicated in the preceding paragraphs, this paper is assuming, at least as a working hypothesis, that Zo is the name of the proto-tribe, from which all the tribes of Zo ancestry have sprung. It is therefore an attempt at delving into Zo cultures and languages in relation other nearby cultures and languages, rather than at describing the state of intra-Zo group of sub-cultures and languages. In other words, it would be worthwhile to view Zo culture and languages from the angle of their possible links with those of 'non-Zos'.

Zo Culture in Relation to Others

The way of life of Zo people has been deeply influenced by Christianity during the last hundred years, as Buddhism did in our neighboring regions in Myanmar, Thailand and China in centuries earlier. There is no discernible Buddhist influence on Zo culture. This has at least two important implications: 1) The Zos might have migrated out of the regions of Buddhist influence before or not long after the arrival of that religion, and moved to areas beyond its reach or to their present locations; but there are no traces of ancient human habitation on their current locations. 2) Then, the Zo tribe might have tended to live in isolation on the fringes of the realm of the civilizations with which they came into contact. The second possibility is likely, considering that Zo tribe has been able to preserve its distinct identity through the midst of history, without the aid of the written word and a relatively advanced material culture. In order to remain intact as a distinct group, they must therefore have kept themselves as apart as feasible, interacting with their neighbors essentially to the extent necessary for their welfare and survival. This would require, among others, avoidance of conflict with more powerful tribes, in the process of which they could be wiped out or absorbed into another larger group. No wonder that even after arriving in the northern Myanmar plains, they remained untouched by the sophisticated Buddhist ideals or way of life. This could also explain the insular world in which the British found the Zos in the late 19th century.

Despite this isolation and apparent lack of substantive intercourse with other peoples for long periods of time, the Zos did develop and adopt a set of concepts as guiding principles for the effective management of society. The application of these principles for running their societies, even more than the strategy of relative isolation mentioned earlier, could have been the reason behind their ability to preserve a distinct identity as a tribe for so long. Let us take, for example, a few well-known principles, which were practiced and preserved in all Zos societies:

1. Respect for elders/seniors and teachers (wise ones);
2. Recognition and acceptance of one's status in life and the duties therewith. Duties enjoined on and rights granted to a Zo boy/youth, a young man (tlangval) and an elder (upa/val upa) by the Zawlbuk system and thereafter are too well known to be recounted here. This system of 'status in life' should not be confused with the system and vertically stratified societies elsewhere.
3. The cultivation of the spirit of selflessness, charity or self-sacrifice, described in Mizo as "Tlawmngaihna";
4. System of administration by the chief or ruler through a council of largely representative advisers/ elders;
5. Protection of their villages or domains by a band of warriors (pasaltha), who were regarded as standard bearers and worthy of emulation;

The last two (4 and 5) practices are fairly common among primitive communities before they encounter modern ideas of administration. The first three concepts are, however, remarkably Confucian and sophisticated in their philosophical and sociological implications. The teachings that one should realise one's status/place in life/society, adhere to it and perform the duties therewith, and that one should respect one's elders/teachers are valid and living ideas for the regulation of an orderly society, probably first propounded and propagated by Confucius in China in late 5th century BC. Confucianism exerted widespread influence in China and other east Asian countries like Japan, Korea, Taiwan and Vietnam, but not so markedly in countries such as Cambodia, Laos, Thailand, Indonesia, Malaysia, the Phillipines and Myanmar. That these principles were some of the fundamental and distinctive features of Zo society has a significance both historically and culturally.

The concept of "Tlawmngaihna" or selflessness/charity appears to be even more of a far-reaching significance. The manifestation of Tlawmngaihna in the conduct of a person has often been described in details, but the writer has not come across any attempt as elaborating the philosophical and ethical assumption behind the concept. The term "Tlawmngaihna' is itself a description/explanation of the ideal or principle, not the name of the idea. A tlawmngai person does his duties, to the best of his ability, without expecting any reward, tangible or intangible, even in the face of certain death. His duties can be described, depending on the circumstances in which he finds himself, but it is not possible to make an exhaustive list of the duties or tasks a tlawmngai person should do. It may be a case of a young man, who saved a colleague's life in a war, a case of a child who lost his life while trying to save a drowning playmate, or a girl who went hungry for sparing food for a sick friend. Situation in which tlawmngaihna may be practiced cannot be completely catalogued, for it is impossible to compile a list of situations in which human beings may find themselves in relation to fellow human beings. What this means is that what impels a person to be tlawmngai towards his fellow human beings is his attitude towards his fellow beings, his attitude to life, his philosophy of life, as it were. This attitude can be most aptly expressed by the word, love - a word perhaps most elaborately understood in Christian Zoram today - love for fellow human beings, or goodwill towards all men. Thus, 'Love thy neighbour more than thou loves thyself or, at least to, thy utmost capacity' - is the philosophy and moral principle, the philosophy of tlawmngaihna, which our ancestors bequeathed to us. It is indeed a message and a teaching as profound and valid as any, one may find anywhere in any age.

This is not the place for a lengthy exposition on the concept of tlawmngaihna, nor can it be treated adequately in a seminar paper. The reason for explaining the concept at some length is to enable us to demonstrate the amazing similarity between it and the core teaching of Confucius (551-479 BC). The key concept to his teachings is the Chinese character or word jen, which has been variously translated as love, virtue, magnanimity, or human heartedness. Several disciples are said to have asked Confucius about the meaning of jen, his briefest answer was "Love men". An ancient Chinese commentary says, "Jen is to love men joyously and from the innermost of one's heart". The central theme of the message of Confucius can be summarized thus - Jen is inborn in all men, an to nurture and cultivate this seed-essence of humanity into full, flowering virtue is the common mission of human life. His teaching has been subsequently regarded as having religious aspects as well, and was later treated as a religion by some followers. For the present purpose, it is sufficient to highlight the close similarities between the essence of the concept of tlawmngaihna and of the teaching of Confucius, and between that of the conduct expected of the practitioners of tlawmngaihna and of the adherents of Confucian thought. In both cases, the life to be led by the practitioners is a life of utter selflessness, in disregard of one's own welfare and at the risk often of one's own safety.

What then is the significance of the parallel between these two teachings? Did the ancestors of the Zos develop this thought independently or could they have learned it from China at some point of time in history? Or are they identical in origin and essence? A definite answer to these questions is impossible today, with the materials available with us. Another significant fact is: among peoples in our neighboring regions such as the Burmese, Thais, etc., who might have at some stage in history migrated from or through some parts of China, there is no tradition of such a pronounced and universal emphasis on tlawmngaihna as it was with our forebears, who on the other hand seem to have adhered to it and cultivated it with near religious fervor. Have their later day religions, such as Buddhism and Islam, swept if off their traditions, as the advent of Christianity almost wiped out our age-old traditions including the sense of tlawmngaihna? Could it be that the Zo ancestors were part and parcel of the Chinese society at one time or, in any case, mingled with the Chinese for long enough to be imbued with their then moral tradition permanently? In either case, they could have found the concept appealing and practical, and adopted it as a guiding principle for the conduct of their society. Subsequently, as seemed to have happened to many of the stories about the origin of their ancient traditions and practices, including the Chhinlung legend, the origin of the concept of tlawmngaihna, if at all known by them, had been possibly neglected and forgotten by the old Zos, who did not feel the urge to explain its origin as long as it worked for them. After all, they claimed to have "lost" the written word, by the wayside, with which to record what had passed before them.

The history of a people in the olden times, unless they are forced to move by invasion or natural calamity, consists mainly in a movement from one pasture to a greener or a safer pasture. In the course of these movements, old and atrophied practices are discarded and what is useful is adapted to new conditions. For instance, the technique for making clothes and shelter, and the means of eking out livelihood undergo intermittent changes. This is a story of technological evolution, and the way primitive communities, regardless of their geographical locations, cope with it is remarkably similar. These elements of physical culture are therefore not reliable sources for determining the past linkages of peoples and their cultures. What can be relied upon, for this purpose, are the ideas that help them to regulate their societies and sustain them to survive. That is the reason why this paper has dwelt at great length with the interesting ideological linkage of Confucian China and Zo philosophical tradition.

Zo languages and the Chinese

The means for articulating the ideas/principles that bind peoples together and enable them sustain their society and survive, and for transmitting these ideas on to new generations is 'language', which is another important marker of linkages of peoples and their cultures. Language also changes, in accord with the changing environment it has to express, but its basic structure and building block do not seem to undergo radical changes unless it is absorbed by a more comprehensive language system. What might have been the basic or proto-Zo language has now branched out into several dialects, but it does not require a laborious research to establish that these dialects are of a common origin. A comparison between the Chinese language (mandarin) and the various Zo dialects* could, perhaps, be of some use in the search for the possible common origin of these dialects.

According to scholarly discipline in linguistics, comparison between two language groups, particularly with a view as

---

* An explanatory note must be inserted here. Mandarin, the language of officials (*guanhua*) has now been adopted as the '*pu tung hua*,' common language or '*guo yu*,' national language, while there are important and phonetically different dialects like Wu (including Sanghai dialect), Hunanese, Cantonese and Hakka. The writer is not conversant with these dialects, and the comparison drawn here is between Mandarin and primarily Mizo (Lusei dialect), as the writer does not have sufficient materials in Zo dialects other than in which he is proficient. Above all, this whole paper should be regarded as a tentative pointer to further research.

to whether they are of a common origin or of the same kind, or closely related, can be drawn in regard to, among others, their structure (morphology), tonality (phonemic or accentuation system), word order (syntax) and phonological correspondence (shared vocabulary with corresponding sounds). Following is an attempt at such a comparison between Zo languages and Mandarin:

1. *Monosyllability (structure):* One of the most distinctive characteristics of all the Zo dialects is that they are monosyllabic; almost every sound they pronounce in their language has a meaning and therefore constitutes a word. this is the same in Chinese (Mandarin), where most of the syllables have meaning and are represented by word-symbols or characters.

Sino-Tibetan group of languages are generally regarded as having this common feature, but mandarin and Zo languages appear to be exceptional in this respect. Any complex or compound word is formed by the combination of these syllable-words. The meaning of the combined word may not be the same as the combined syllables; instead, the newly formed word is usually to express a more complex idea. For example, hmangaihna (love in Mizo) is a combination of hma+ngai, followed by the abstraction suffix 'na' while its Chinese equivalent, aiqing (pronounced as aih-chhing) is = ai (love) + qing (feeling) or felt love, indicating between man and woman.

2. *Tonality:* Each Chinese vowel as in Zo language has a certain tone (thluk) of voice. Standard Mandarin has four tones. These tones can be adopted without any modification in Zo, as demonstrated in the following explanation of the tonal system of Mandarin. The Zo syllable – pa is used for the tone indicator. The first tone, marked ( ) is called level tone; it is spoken in a high pitch and neither rises nor falls, as pa (buhzem or rice storage). The second, ( ), is called rising tone; it starts with a lower voice and ends up high as pa (fungi or as pa in mau-pa). The

third, ( ), is called low tone. The voice is dropped at first and then rises, as pa (masculine, manly or male). And the fourth, ( ), is called falling tone. The voice falls from high to low, as with pa (father). There are a number of syllables that are slight in sound and are called toneless or neutral tones, and are not marked, as chak (strong), fak (praise), lem (fake or look-alike), pet (bite), mit (eye), kut (hand), etc.

The importance of these tones is that without using them, both Chinese and Zo sentences are virtually unintelligible. In the case of Chinese, each syllable is represented by a character, e.g., man ( ). If a boy learns the word or character, man, he automatically learns it with its tone, because there are no other characters in Chinese, which look like the symbol for man. Whereas in Zo, as the tones are not marked, one has to guess or find it out from the context or meaning of the whole sentence. For instance, *"Tur tui in turin min tur a, a zuang tur tur mai"* can be read correctly only by a native speaker or one who knows the meaning beforehand, i.e., "He urges me to drink poisoned water, and jumps up and down, or jumps *tur tur*." The same is true of Mandarin, if it is written in Roman letters without tone marks. The syllable, *shi*, for example, can mean either *is, lion, ten, or stone,* depending on the tones. Now, it seems clear that both Mandarin and Zo language cannot be understood properly without the tones, which are exactly four in number in both cases.

3. *Syntax*: The word order in Mandarin is subject-verb-object, (like in English), while in Zo dialects, it is usually object-subject-verb. *Wo chi fan or I eat rice or Chaw ka ei*. In addressing a second person, however, it is the same as mandarin or English, e.g. *I love you, Wo ai ni,* or *Ka ngai (hmangaih) che*. There are traces of word order in old Chinese similar to those in Zo dialects. The word sequence in Tai and Karen group is like Mandarin, but Tai and Karen are conclusively considered divergent from

Chinese. Similarity word order is not regarded by linguists as key element for determining genetic relation of languages.

There is neither time nor space for comparison of Zo language to Mandarin by detailed analysis of their respective syntaxes. There are, however, some interesting similarities in arrangement of words between the two:

Where "*chi*" is used in Zo to denote type or sort, as in *ei-chi, in-chi,* (eatable type, drink type) the Chinese use '*zi or ji*', but they also use '*zi/ji*' in a variety of ways to particularize nouns. A Zo suffix '*-tu*' as in ziaktu, phuahtu, eptu, etc., has a Chinese equivalent in '*tze*', which is used mainly for professionals like news reporter, writer, sportsman, etc. In more complex and elaborate description of things or persons, '*thil*' and '*mi*' (*dong-si* and *ren*) are used rather freely, as in '*ei leh bar thil and ziak leh chhiar thiam mi*', not as *ei leh bar chi and ziak leh chhiar thiamtu*'. An important divergence between these two languages is the positioning of the qualifiers of nouns - e.g., *big man, good man* in Chinese are *man big, man good* in Zo. Another Zo word (*ta*), meaning 'to own' has a Chinese equivalent in '*de*', pronounced as short *da*, and its usage is like that of Zo. Whose is this? - *hei hi tu ta nge* or *zhei shi shei de*?- is answered as *ka ta, I ta,* and *a ta, Lala ta* etc., or *wo de, ni de, tha de, Lala de,* etc. There are of course other situations in which this word is extensively used as a conjunctive qualifier. An instance of similarity in the concept of the formation of compound words may be added. Take 'ming' or 'hming/ ming' in Zo. Famous becomes 'yao-ming' or 'ming-thang', and so on.

4. *Phonological Correspondence:* This is considered to be the most important element for determining the genetic relationship of languages. What it really means is common vocabulary with corresponding sound, not necessarily the same. Following are what the writer found at random, without any systematic research; and there could be many

more. They are mainly illustrative. (Detailed study in this field is required):

(1) Words with institutional or ideological implications:- "*T'ien*", pronounced as "thien" in Hmar and Lai, in old Chinese means "god, or heavenly god". In modern Chinese, it now generally means heaven, sky, or day, but is still used to mean 'god' in non-religious sense- *t'ien a*! is used as an exclamatory 'my god!'. Thus, "pathian" in Zo means "father god". The equivalent of "chibai" in Zo is "libai" in Chinese, and it is used exclusively to mean "to worship". In old Tedim dialect, "mang" means "king or lal or chief," and in Chinese, king or chief is "wang". The replacement of soft consonant like "w" or "y" by "m" and "v" or "h" seems common. For instance, "wai" (outside) or "wai(z)" (outsider or foreigner) possibly became "vai" meaning outsiders or aliens, "yuan" is turned into "huan" (yard or garden), "yong" becomes "hmang" (use).

(2) Equivalent words or closely corresponding in sound and meaning between Zo and Mandarin, selected at random for illustration: (The transliteration of the Chinese works used in the following is not the standard form. They are written in Mizo system to convey the sound closest to the original, while *tr* is used as 't' with a dot underneath).

Numeral in Cantonese dialect is particularly close to Zo dialects. Yat (khat), yi (hnih, ni (Paite), sam (thum), li (li), 'ng (nga), luk (ruk, guk), chat (sarih, sagih), pat (riat, giat), ku (kua, kuo) and sap (sawm). The system of counting after ten is also the same in both languages, that is, by adding number one to nine after ten and so on. Thus, twenty is 'two-ten', thirty, 'three-ten, and so on even after hundred. The year 1999 is counted as one thousand, nine hundred, ten-nine and nine.

Chinese	*Zo dialect*	*English meaning*
mang	mang	dream
thing	ding	stop or park
thrang	thrang	to grow (person)
chou	chie (Thado)	walk or go
shi	shi (Lai)	is or to be
hao	hoih (Paite/Thado)	well or good
pu	puo (Thado)	no, not
mei	mawi	beautiful
ming	ming (Paite/Thado)	name
nai	nai (Paite)	milk
niu	nu	female
mei	kei (Paite)	not
hai mei	nai kei (Paite)	not yet
shuo	sawi	tell, say
zui (chui)	rui	drunk
jiu (chiu)	zu	wine
thru (chhu)	chhuak	out/get out
kou or ko	kua or kuo (Hmar)	hole/mouth
ruh/ru	lut	enter
ruh kou	luh-ka	entrance
xin/shin zhong	thinlung	deep in heart/mind
xin/shin li	thinlai	- do -
han	hua	hate
zuo/chuo	chuang	ride
ching / chhing	hring	green / fresh
chhai	thlai	vegetables
khuai / kuai	thuai / thuai thuai	quick / quickly
chong	ching (thlai)	plant / sow
dang dang	dang dang	etc., etc.
yi-yang (i-iang)	in ang	same, similar
chan mei	chawimawi	praise / glorify
zhei / chei	hei	this, here

chei/zhei yang	hetiang	like this, this way
na	kha	there
sui/shui	tui	water
trih	hria/hrie(Hmar)	know
chiu/jiu	(chiuh)chiah/chieh (Hmar)	just, only chui/
zhui	chhui/sui (Hmar)	chase, trace, pursue
aih/ai	ai/aih (exclamation)	disagree
threng	thrang	to increase
au, ao	awm, mung	to cook, boil slowly
ma ?	maw ?	interrogative particle
a, a ?	a, a ?	mid-sentence, question particles
bie-shi	beisei	hope, expect
shiang	suan (Paite)	think
kan	kang, ro	dry (of water)
hua (r)	par	flower
ji-ji, ji-deh	chhinchhiah	remember, recall
truh	thru (t)	reside, to settle
guh, kuh	ruh, guh (Paite)	bone
chhing	chiang, chieng (Hmar)	clear (understand)
man, manh	muang	slow (ly)
nun, nan	no	tender
du(z)	dul	abdomen
pha	phu (hlau)	fear
ban-lai	hmanlai, atir-in	originally
hah-chi	hah-chhiau	sneeze
wang, uangh	mang (nghilh)	forget
ri(h)	ni	sun

Conclusion

What has been attempted in this paper is to provide some data, strongly suggestive of possible linguistic and cultural links between the Zo people and China. The Zos have survived this long as a people with distinctive culture and languages. With thorough research, it ought to be possible to establish the nature of their connection with other peoples in the past. The paucity of records and convincing materials currently at hand should not deter us from this challenge. In other words, we should not be satisfied with exercises in conjecture, based on a few discursive old terms or legends. Obviously, much need to be investigated beyond the range of this paper. As for this paper, if it is considered persuasive enough to inspire further research in its direction, its purpose will have been achieved.

A further research will have to include a compilation of old Zo vocabulary, terms and traditions for comparison with Mandarin and the various Chinese dialects, both old and new. Old Chinese folklores, their traditional sports and play, entertainments etc., will have to be gone into, and compared with those of the Zos.

3

A MIZO PHILOSOPHICAL HERITAGE: TLAWMNGAIHNA OR SELFLESSNESS[1] THEN AND NOW

Introduction

The philosopher Bertrand Russell wrote, (our) "conceptions of life and the world which we call 'philosophical' are a product of two factors: one, inherited *ethical* and *religious* conceptions; the other, the sort of *investigation* which may be called 'scientific,' using this word in its broadest sense. Individual philosophers have differed widely in regard to the pro-portions in which these factors entered into their systems, but it is the presence of both, in some degree, that characterizes philosophy."[2] Indeed, philosophy, from the earliest times, has been an integral part of the life of the community, not merely a matter of disputation between a few learned men of different schools of thought. In other words, where there is a community there is a philosophy. By using the word 'philosophy' in this very wide sense, we do not need to take up the circuitous task of establishing that there is such a thing as the Mizo philosophical heritage.

Bertrand Russell also asked, among others, "Is there a way of living that is noble? If there is a way of living that is noble, in what does it consist, and how shall we achieve it?" And he continued, "The studying of these questions, if not the answering of them, is the business of philosophy." This essay is an attempt to explain that the concept of *tlawmngaihna* and the practice of it are our ancestors' answers to Russell's questions. To put it in another way, the concept of *tlawmngaihna* is the ethical component of the Mizo philosophical heritage. We shall also deal with the questions: how has this concept fared in the way of living of Mizos today, if not very well (as most discerning observers appear to contend), and why? (I am using in most cases the plural pronouns "we" and "our" in order to engage the reader in a dialogue as a co-explorer of the ideas I am trying to articulate).

I have also avoided recounting of old stories and legends which are regarded as demonstrating that *tlawmngaihna* was indeed the moral precept that guided our forebears. The essay could, therefore, be a little mystifying for some one who is unfamiliar with the legends and folklores of the Mizos. However, as it will be presently made clear, there is no longer any doubt that the Mizos assumed this concept to be the guiding principle of their way of life, a sort of a philosophy of life, as it were. And it does not appear to be necessary to try and reestablished it as such.

A Definition

Whenever we speak of our cultural traits, the first and foremost quality we usually point out is *tlawmngaihna*. However, when it comes to defining the concept, we often explain it variously, as can be seen from the following selected examples:

1. Zairema (Rev): literally translated it as "an unwillingness to be defeated or be beaten." He also defined it as "Mizo *dharma*." (Bangalore Mizo Christian Fellowship Publication).
2. R. Vanlawma: called it "a heart-felt desire to serve and work for others." (Zorimawi YK2 Issue).
3. J. Lalsangzuala: explained it as "the spirit of selfless service to others and a noble zeal to stand by those who need help." (Mizoram Millennium Souvenir).
4. Lalkhama called it, "Mizo ethos, ... ideal conduct

and standard of behaviour." (Mizoram Millennium Souvenir).

5. K. C. Lalvunga: defined it as "an innate goodness of man which manifests in good deeds in all sorts of way." (Zikpuii Pa Hnuhma).

There is no need for elaborating further that all the above mentioned definitions are applicable to the concept of *tlawmngaihna*. All of us, I think, would recognize a *tlawmngai* person whenever we see him / her in action. Every act of goodness for others can be regarded as its manifestation. A boy who willingly shares his toys with a friend is a *tlawmngai* child. A girl who offers her seat in a city bus to an old woman is a *tlawmngai* girl. A soldier who gets wounded in a battle while dragging a dying colleague to safety is also such a person. So were the New York firemen who died at the World Trade Center or the young man who sacrificed his seat in a lifeboat for a drowning woman when the *Titanic* sunk in the Atlantic.

We can go on enumerating the situations in which *tlawmngaihna* can be shown by all manners of people of varying ages. The kind of deeds a *tlawmngai* person performs can also vary almost indefinitely. It is not possible to make a complete list of situations in which *tlawmngaihna* may be practiced, just as it is impossible to compile a complete list of circumstances in which human beings may find themselves in relation to fellow human beings. This is because what impels a person to behave *tlawmngai*-ly towards his fellow human beings is his *attitude* to his fellow beings, his attitude to life and, in the ultimate analysis, towards mankind or his conception of the purpose and destiny of human life. In its perfect state, it is nothing less than moral excellence, a condition the Romans called *virtus. It may also be termed as an unconditional concern or love for fellow human beings, or as pure goodwill towards all mankind.* For, a person with such an attitude is supposed to do his chosen duties to the best of his ability, without expecting any rewards, tangible or intangible, regardless of the consequences, even in the face certain death.

Philosophical Assumptions

The conception that the destiny of man is to serve mankind, or that love for fellow human beings is one's mission in life, is obviously derived from certain philosophical assumptions. These assumptions would consist in questions concerning the true nature of the ultimate reality, of mind and man, ideal society, truth and so on. Since we are focused mainly on the ethical aspect of it and its changing role in Mizo society, we shall not delve into these questions. Suffice it to say that the concept of *tlawmngaihna* also has interesting metaphysical implications. (This, indeed, is a fitting subject for further research).

Its Attributes

Before we go on to the application of *tlawmngaihna* in Mizo society, it would be appropriate to try and sort out its main attributes. Our forefathers did not bequeath to us a definition of *tlawmngaihna*, nor did they explain to us the steps that we need go through to achieve it, even if not fully at least in a fair measure. All we know is that they themselves tried to live a life of *tlawmngaihna* to the extent they were capable and that they taught their young by the examples of their life in practice. Although it is primarily an innate goodness, our ancients clearly believed that it can be inculcated and also cultivated. The main purpose behind the institution of *Zawlbuk*, the Bachelors' Dormitory or Quarters, for example, was for training young boys till they attain manhood in the practice of *tlawmngaihna*.

It seems possible, however, to distil from what might be termed as their codes of ethics certain qualities of character, without acquiring or possessing which a person cannot be considered *tlawmngai* or selfless. These are - *rinawmna* (honesty), *huaisenna* (courage), *khawngaihna* (compassion), *taimakna* (diligence), *ngaihdamna* (forgiveness), *dawhtheihna* (tolerance) and *inngaihtlawmna* / *thuhnuairawlhna* (humility). Each of these qualities of character and how it is applied to living can be explained further. For our present purpose, however, it is perhaps enough to assert that it is impossible to imagine a *tlawmngai* person who does not possess these virtues. These virtues may also be described as the steps in the path to *tlawmngaihna.*

Tlawmngaihna and Mizo Society

Before we take up the status of *tlawmngaihna* in today's Mizoram, it would be useful to examine briefly how the Mizos have some how come to associate themselves, even their core culture, with this concept especially. It does not require much imagination to conclude that the kind of goodness this concept implies is valued by all cultures, indeed, by the entire mankind. Yet the Mizos, then and now, have always considered it their special cultural trait. One obvious reason is that in the pre-colonial, pre-writing and pre-Christian era, this concept was our primary, if not the sole, guiding principle for living a "life that is noble." As Zairema has aptly defined it, it deserves to be called 'Mizo *dharma,*' in so far as it was idealized and sought to be applied by our forefathers in their daily lives. Even today, despite our many admitted shortcomings, it is constantly being "talked" about as an ideal to be aspired to.

There is a remarkable similarity between this concept and the core teaching of Confucius (B.C. 551 - 479), which is represented by the Chinese word, *jen or zhen,* variously translated as love, virtue, magnanimity, or human heartedness. To questions about the meaning of *jen,* Confucius was reported to have replied simply, "Love men." The summary of his teaching is: *jen* is inborn in all men, to nurture and cultivate this seed-essence of humanity into full, flowering virtue is the common mission of human life. If Mizos originally came from south-west China, as some historians argued, it is possible that we "learned" it from the Chinese. At any rate, this amazing similarity of "core beliefs" has significance both historically and culturally. Here again, we are moving away from our main theme.

Its Role in Mizoram Today

Among the perceptive observers of the cultural scene in today's Mizoram, there is a near consensus view that the practice of *tlawmngaihna* has steadily declined. There are some alarmists who even warn that our society is heading towards a moral collapse. The noted writer, J. Malsawma once observed, "We are all fakes; we are all wearing masks." If this is the case, it would also mean that we are lacking in most of the attributes of the concept we mentioned earlier, such as honesty, courage, diligence, compassion, forgiveness, tolerance and humility. Is this really the case? Or are we too pessimistic about our situation and future?

Let us begin by examining just the case of *honesty* at an individual level. It seems to me that we have remained quite reliable and often down-to-earth in our individual and social interactions except in circumstances, which are directly connected with *earning of livelihood, religious practices* and *politics*. We are dependable in friendship and make lasting friendship, not just amongst ourselves but also with the so-called outsiders. The very fact that so many of us are 'actively' disturbed by the 'deteriorating' condition of morality in our society is the evidence of our steadfastness to that basic individual simplicity and honesty. In other words, most of us appear to have continued to retain the simplicity and an uncalculating harmlessness, even innocence, which was virtually 'second nature' for our forebears in the more distant and pristine times.

On the other hand, when it comes to our *economic* endeavors and our participation in *politics*, we do not seem to be much disturbed by moral qualms and scruples. It is perhaps pointless to use elaborate arguments to confirm the prevalence of widespread and penetrating corruption in our economic lives and political practices. Surely, this is the reason behind the lack so far in Mizoram of even a single cost-effective infrastructure project. It has also led to transgressions in the practice of our religion. How and why have we become like this? The answers to these questions will have to be sought from our exposure to outside influences. And this is the main relevance of this paper to the theme of the present seminar as well. Outside influences to which we were exposed in the last hundred years or so were: the British colonial administration, Christianity/ Missionaries and post-independence Indian politics.

Colonial Administration

The impact of the *colonial authorities* on Mizo society was mainly political. The first colonial official who commented at some length on Mizo society was perhaps H. T. Lewin. He was so impressed with the social order he found at the village level in Mizoram that he admiringly wrote, "We are acquainted with Plato's *Republic*, with Sydney's *Utopia*, with Bacon's *New Atlantis*, and later, Compte's *Philosophical Positif* - dreams these, all of them; - the ideas of eminent men as to the conditions which should exist in this world, as to the social relations among their fellows, which are the most conducive to happiness, but here among these hill tribes we find an actual existing system in practical working, which might well be classed among the visions of Utopian philosophy...Their mode of government may be described as democracy tempered by despotism."[3] This was 20 years before Christian missionaries arrived in Mizoram. H. T. Lewin might have overstated his appreciation of the Mizo society and romanticized it a little, I am not aware of any observation made by colonial officers on pre-writing Mizo society, which is not positive. In fact, A. Mackenzie appreciatively and extensively quoted him in his book, 'The North East Frontier of India' while J. Shakespeare dedicated to him his book *'The Lushei Kuki Clans'*.

The main objective of the colonial administration was to maintain peace and order amongst hitherto, at times, feuding chiefs and villages, while ensuring their loyalty to the British Empire. One set of the duties of the Superintendent, the then district officer, testifies to this. "His duties are to settle all disputes between chief and chief, village and village, and tribe and tribe, and to prevent all public breaches of peace.

He will not interfere in the administration of each village by its own chief unless in very exceptional cases when called on to interfere by either the chief or the villagers, and then only on strong grounds being shown, and he shall report all such cases to the Commissioner."[4] As their policy was guided by the principle of the least interference in local practices and customs, their direct influence on culture might have been largely benign. By ensuring peace and tranquility in the entire land and, through the network of their administration, by providing linkages / interactions among hitherto relatively isolated communities, they could have also contributed to the growth and nurture of a homogenous culture. (This is another topic needing further research).

The British officers did show their concern for the wellbeing of Mizo society by drastic intervention in exceptional circumstances. The District Superintendent, N. E. Parry banished some prostitutes in the mid-1920s while his successor, A. G. McCall expelled Laldela of Kulikawn from Mizoram in the early 30s for attempting to submit a memorandum to the Simon Commission proposing that Lushai Hills should be included in 'India proper,' not in the "Excluded Areas." McCall also put down "a hysterical" revivalist Christian movement at Kelkang village in 1938 and transferred a PWD official, Rualkhuma, to North East Frontier Ahministration (NEFA), now Arunachal, for taking part in that revival.[5] The indirect but decisive and durable impact they made on Mizo society was by 'facilitating' the introduction of Christianity in Mizoram. The question whether the colonial authorities 'actively' encouraged the missionaries or were indifferent to them can be controversial, and requires careful research. N. E. Parry, for one, was very critical of those missionaries who taught their followers to abandon their customary practices, including drinking of alcoholic beverages.[6]

Christianity

The impact of Christianity, or of its institutional embodiment, the Church, on Mizo society could only be described as 'total'; but we are here concerned only with its possible influences on the traditional ethical practice of the society or the ethical aspect of our culture. As another paper is being presented on the over all role of the Church in the evolving Mizo society, I shall not go into details of how the Church developed, obviously unwittingly at least in the initial stages, into an institution behind which the morally unsound could also take shelter, thereby providing an instrument by which hypocrisy could be effectively practiced.

Before the advent of Christianity, social life and social interaction were essentially transparent. In every *Veng* or community of a part of the village, everyone knew who was upright or untrustworthy. There was no way a liar or a dishonest person could pass himself off as anything other than how he was known by the community. If, however, some one claims that he is a born-again Christian and is actively involved in Church work now-a-days, and if he is also approved by the Church leaders as such, he has to be regarded as a devout. While there is no doubt that many of such persons are genuine believers and truly devout, the fact remains that there is now scope for "pretenders" involving a mechanism of "approval" under the authority of the Church. We need not attempt to count the number of such "pretenders" today. And this is one aspect of our modern day culture which has a harmful effect on the practice of the concept of *tlawmngaihna*. N. E. Parry bluntly stated as early as in 1932, "No one can pretend that it is a good thing that *tawmngaihna*, while still practiced by heathen Lusheis, should be conspicuous by its absence among Christian Lushei communities; the reverse should be the case."[7]

Politics

Mizo Union: The first political party in Mizoram was founded on April 9, 1946 and was named the *Mizo Common People's Union,* reflecting the anti-Chiefs sentiments of the common people. Though its name was later changed to *Mizo Union,* it remained a party of the common people. The Mizo Union soon came into conflict with Superintendent L. L.

Peters, who was arguing for the continuation of the leading role of the Chiefs in the future setup of the administration for the district. The Mizo Union then launched a non-cooperation movement in December, 1948, which lasted till February, 1949 and demanded the abolition of Chieftaincy. Though meant to be non-violent, the demonstrations that accompanied the movement were at times brutally violent against the Chiefs and their advisers as also against whom they regarded as supporters of the Chiefs such as Zalen Pawl or members of the United Mizo Freedom Organization (UMFO), a faction of Mizo Union, which broke away from the party over the issue of joining the Union of Burma, instead of the Indian Union. The demonstrators stoned houses of their opponents and destroyed several properties.[8]

Thus, the first mass movement in Mizoram politics was emotional, irrational and divisive of the Mizo society. It was tinged with hatred and envy, and was directed primarily against the Chiefs and their advisers, the custodians of tradition and, in particular, the custodians of traditional social mores. It also brought with it a way of thinking that assumes political activity to be essentially a freewheeling exercise, an approach which is now flourishing in Mizoram. With the removal of the Chiefs and the installation of Village Councils in their place, there was not only a sudden break in our traditional governance but we were also subjected to a rule by inexperienced and untrained people. The tradition of leadership by competence and born-leaders was replaced at one stroke by a system of election, which, as it has turned out, is prone to corruption and ineptitude.

What is perhaps more damaging is that the Mizo Union also introduced a practice in Mizoram for the first time what is now generally termed as *corruption*. After the abolition of chieftaincy, once the party captured the District Council, the allotment of housing plots in the towns was monopolized by members of the Mizo Union. Jobs under the Council and Teachers of Primary Schools, which came under the authority of the Council, were practically reserved for members of the party. In fact, the lowering of the qualities of teachers and of teaching in the Primary Schools begun in this period and the Mizo Union was responsible for these. What is surprising was that no widespread and vocal protests were made at the time against this unjust and partisan practice by the Mizo Union. Participation in party politics has since been regarded as one of the means of earning livelihood or of enriching oneself.

MNF: The Mizo National Front (MNF) came into being and became the main rival of the Mizo Union, then the largest political party. (For our present purpose, there is no need to discuss the merits or demerits of the policies of the MNF.) Once the MNF resorted to insurgency, the rivalry between the two parties was further compounded. For the first time in our history, the idea of killing a fellow Mizo over differences in politics became somehow 'acceptable' and was even selectively practiced. Those who did not believe in the 'cause of Mizo independence' did not dare to speak up and could not oppose the insurgency, for fear of their lives. The common people were placed at the crossfire between the security forces and the insurgents, as it was said, between the hammer and the anvil. They were faced all too often by a situation where so many of them could no longer afford to be 'honest'. The insurgency then 'provoked' a particularly brutal and unprecedented response from the Security Forces, which was the decision to set up *Grouping Centers* for the scattered villages.

The impact of this measure on Mizo society is also yet to be properly assessed. What can be generally said is that, if it did not destroy, it certainly disrupted the fundamental fabrics of our society. Before then, the village communities were like extended families, with their lives interwoven in all sorts of ways. It was at the village that the traditional values had been developed, nurtured and kept alive over the years.[9] At the Grouping Centers, hitherto strangers to one another became neighbors, and even rival villages were crowded into the same community. It would have felt strange to live in a grouped village, which belonged to no one or in which no one felt belong to. For, it was the *sense of belonging to a familiar community* that made the Mizo villager tick and hum. In such confusing circumstances, added to the constant pressures of economic hardship and tense security situation, it is possible to imagine, the villager would have been suspicious of his neighbors and cared less about things like minor thefts, lazy and lax sexual tendencies among the youth, dishonest behavior of others and so on. In short, when taking care of one's self interest with cunning became about the most effective means of survival for one's family, it would have been extremely difficult for him to try and adhere steadfastly to the fine qualities of character we have cited in the foregoing as embodying the concept of *tlawmngaihna*.

Party Politics and Public Life

We have seen how the Mizo Union turned participation in party politics into a paying proposition at the first opportunity, that is, as soon as it became the ruling party in the district council. This trend was substantially reinforced by the entry into Mizoram of the Indian National Congress (I) when that party contested the elections to the Legislative Assembly of the then Union Territory of Mizoram in 1972. For the first time, a fleet of jeeps and a large amount of money were brought into Mizoram for use by the Congress (I) in the election campaigns. Till then, election campaigns were drab affairs. No one would have imagined that lakhs of rupees could be spent on elections.[10] Before, candidates would serve red tea to the crowd in their campaign meetings and entertain people, narrating their own acclaimed and perceived merits or the alleged shortcomings of their opponents.

Upon that election, the first UT government was formed by the Mizo Union, which before long merged with the Indian National Congress. Once Mizoram became a centrally administered territory, with development funds pouring in from the Centre, corruption gradually became part of the political practice in the state. That corruption has become rampant today in most branches of the state administration needs no elaboration. What is morally pernicious, however, is that most of us have become indifferent to this state of affairs and have begun to take it for granted as if it had become a norm in officialdom and in our dealings with officials. The "religious" amongst us are no different. Indeed, corruption can no longer be associated with any particular political party; it has permeated the whole society and is now embedded in the system of governance and public life.

The result is that most of us are now living double lives with double standards. In our private lives, we continue to invoke outwardly our traditional values and virtues whereas in public life we tolerate all sorts of irregularities. This sort of notion of split morality can only serve as a justification or pretext for living an unwholesome life. Morality cannot be compartmentalized. At any rate, the attitude to living such a notion implies is completely at variance with the concept of *tlawmngaihna*. Nor is the moral atmosphere it generates conducive to the practice of *tlawmngaihna*.

To recap our arguments, the advent of Christianity, with its rejection of our customary and traditional practices, unwittingly discouraged the practice of *tlawmngaihna*. In its current state, as it is actually used by a large number of its members, the Church is amenable to be abused by hypocritical "pretenders" as a moral smokescreen.[11] This has led and is leading to the spread of hypocrisy in our midst, which is diametrically opposed to the concept of selflessness.

In politics, rigid partisanship has so far prevented healthy democracy from taking a firm root in Mizoram. Many participants in party politics tended to regard politics as a means of eking out livelihood. This has naturally resulted in the prevalence of corruption in public life. Religiosity in appearance and form goes well with our corrupt public life. We have thus transformed the ways in which we practice our religion and politics into hindrances to the nurture of *tlawmngaihna* in our society.

REFERENCES

1. There is no exact English equivalent to denote the conceptual connotation of Tlawmngaihna.
2. Russell, Bertrand: *History of Western Philosophy*, George Allen & Unwin Ltd, London, 1975, pp. 13
3. Herbert Thomas Lewin, Deputy Commissioner, Chittagong Hills, Colloquial Exercises on the Lushai Dialect, 1874. He went on to observe that even though chieftaincy was hereditary, succession to it was only for those born leaders who had the capacity to retain the loyalties of their "perfectly free" subjects.
4. Sir Robert Reid, *History of Frontier Areas bordering on Assam*, pp. 30. (Rules made in 1891).
5. Sir Robert Reid, *ibid*. pp. 47 and interview with Rev. Zairema on 12. 4. 2006. Rualkhuma is Zairem's father. The revivalists preached that the second coming of Christ was about to take place and the end of the world was imminent.. They refused to work and cooperate with their Chief saying that the British Empire was going to end soon. Earlier, an Inquiry Commission was set up to look into the Maharaja of Tripura's claim that the territory of Lushai Hills west of Tlawng or Dhaleshwari river belonged to his kingdom. N. E. Perry told all the Brus living in the area to tell the Commission that they were 'Pachuau", a Mizo clan. As the result, the territory was awarded to Mizoram.
6. *The Lakhers*, N. E. Parry, 1932, Part I.
7. N.E. Parry, *The Lakhers*, 1932, pp.23.
8. As the son of a Treasurer of Mizo Union party in his village, the writer also took part in the demonstrations.
9. The Japanese and the Koreans are acutely aware of this. That is why they have adopted various measures to preserve their traditional village life alongside modernization.
10. I do not know how much money was brought by Bihar MP Mr. Jyaji on that occasion. I did see two gunny bags of cash being counted by him and Mr. Hrangchhuana, Congress (I) President at the residence of the Cheif Commissioner, S. J. Das, who confirmed to me that the money was meant for election campaign.
11. In an opinion survey, Zozam Times asked its readers if they believed that the recent Revival Centenary at Vaivakawn would help improve the spiritual life of the participants. 98 % of the respondents said, "No". Zozam Times of 24. 4. 2006.

4

NEGOTIATING WITH INSURGENCY AND HOLDING ON TO PEACE: The Mizoram Experience

Introduction

Of the few detailed narratives available in English about the insurgency movement launched by the Mizo National Front (MNF) on February 28 1966, there is not one that has been written from experience by a prominent participant in the movement. A few books by such participants have recently been published in Mizo language. Even some of these books appear to have been written not entirely as objective records of events but with some political points of view in mind. A reluctance to 'expose' former underground colleagues may also be inhibiting.

An attempt at a study of any aspects of the MNF insurgency movement, therefore, continues to face the problem of the lack of reliable and non-speculative materials. And the demanding exercise of personal interviews with the original participants, in this case, in the peace initiatives in the early stages of the insurgency is a necessity.

The Genetic Dichotomy of the MNF

In order to understand the process of the negotiations that culminated in the signing of the Peace Accord on 30 June 1986 between the MNF and the Government of India, it seems necessary to first delve into some aspects of the nature of the insurgency movement as well as the probable motivations of its prime initiators. In this process, the reasons why the Accord lasts in Mizoram may also become apparent, if not fully, at least partially.

`There is a view rather prevalent in Mizoram today that the MNF leadership, particularly the late Laldenga had not actually intended to lead the MNF party into insurgency whereas the bulk of the MNF cadres, especially the young intellectual elite[1] and the less educated believed in the cause of 'independence' for Mizoram and were prepared for a protracted struggle for it. Often quoted in support of this view is the statement Laldenga made in what may be termed as the pre-insurgency 'peace talks' with the Mizo Union party leaders, Ch. Chhunga (L) and C. Pahlira in mid December 1965. He was quoted to have said, "Even if we decide to change our plan (rebellion), our boys will kill us. You will have to understand our predicament." After explaining his views on the impossibility of secession from the Indian Union and the sufferings that rebellion would bring to the innocent people in Mizoram, Ch. Chhunga was said to have replied, "If Zoram (*Mizoram*) can be saved from trouble by the death of Laldenga and Chhunga, we should both be ready to make the sacrifice."[2]

The former Mizo Union leader, C. Pahlira's assessment was that the then Chief Minister of Assam, B. P. Chaliha was trying to use Laldenga and his party as an instrument to destroy Mizo Union, which was the ruling party then in the District Council of Mizoram.[3] In a memorandum submitted to Prime Minister Indira Gandhi on 22 June 1966, the Mizo Union leaders also openly accused Chaliha of having given "active and material support to MNF."[4] Apart from his political ambitions, Laldenga of course had his personal grouse against the District Council, from the services of which he had resigned as an accounts official upon being investigated on charges of embezzlement. The treatment meted out by the Assam Government to the secret visit to East Pakistan of Laldenga, MNF Vice President Lalnunmawia and Sainghaka, later MNF Home Minister, in early December 1963 was rather lenient. Laldenga and Lalnunmawia were arrested on their return on 24 December 1963. Despite the seditious implication of the visit they were released on 14 February 1964 on a written promise that they would confine their political activities within the bounds of the Indian constitution. Laldenga also claimed to have convinced Chaliha then that 'independence' was only his slogan and that his real aim was to capture power in the district council.[5] "Right from the start, the MNF made its military and secessionist intentions very clear. But the Assam Chief Minister willfully chose to ignore it," (Sajal Nag.)[6] Mrs. Laldenga (Biakdiki) was also reported to have said in a speech at a MNF party function commemorating Laldenga's birthday on 11 June 2003 that her husband had aimed to overthrow the District Council, not to plunge Mizoram into bloodshed.[7] The manner in which Chaliha reacted to the news of the outbreak of insurgency in Mizoram seems to fit into this argument. He was said to have screamed, "Laldenga stabbed me on my back!" He also overturned his office desk and abruptly dismissed an ongoing meeting at the mention of Laldenga's "duplicity".[8]

On the other hand, as the result of his 1963-end visit to Dacca, by December 1965, the Inter Services Intelligence (ISI) in East Pakistan had already trained two batches of MNF Volunteers (MNV). With several hundreds more locally trained volunteers, the stage had been set for the MNF rebellion. In other words, those who had joined MNF to 'fight for Mizoram independence' were now ready to strike. Yet, even at the last hours on the 28 February 1966, after the "Zero" hour had been set and volunteers were positioning to strike their appointed targets, there appeared to be signs of wavering on the part of some leaders.

There were two meetings of the MNF leadership at different locations on that night, one for the top leadership and the other for civil leaders such as Senators and high officials, to whom the decision to strike was to be conveyed for the first time. The Senators group sent to the Cabinet group a last minute suggestion to postpone the strike on the ground of suspicion that there had appeared to be a leakage of information about their move. In the Cabinet meeting, J. F. Manliana, Chief Justice and Lallianzuala Sailo, Senate representative spoke at length in favour of postponement. Time was getting late, yet Laldenga would not speak. Defense Minister R. Zamawia finally had to explain the impossibility of postponement at that hour, upon which Laldenga simply said, "Yes".[9] In any case, having jumped into the clutches of the Pakistani ISI, Laldenga could not have avoided creating serious troubles against India at one time or another.

Laldenga left Aizawl on the night of 28 February 1966 and eventually arrived at Dacca with his family and personal staff and took shelter there. He was supposed to campaign from there to enlist support of foreign powers. He returned to Mizoram in December 1966 to attend a parliament session held at Sialsir village from 11 to 15 December and lingered in Mizoram for about a week and returned again to Dacca.[10] At the Sialsir meeting he was virtually "forced"[11] to hand over the powers of the President to Vice President Lalnunmawia. Laldenga's long absences from the scene of action especially during the early stages of insurgency and his manoeuvres to have a grip over the MNF movement by remote control were also complicating factors behind "the widening gap of understanding" between him and most of the educated MNF cadres.[12]

The Seeds of Negotiations and the Role of Church / Civil Society

Apart from the probable attitude of the MNF leadership towards peace settlement that can be inferred from the foregoing, Laldenga's meeting with Rev. Zairema in mid December 1965, a little over two months prior to the start of the rebellion, could be the first definite indication that some of the top leaders did not intend to prolong the insurgency. Laldenga was accompanied by Lalhmingthanga, Foreign Minister and C. Lalkhawliana, Finance Minister, when he personally requested Rev. Zairema to organize a "Peace Mission," once the MNF rose in revolt, along the same line as that had been set up in Nagaland. At this meeting,

Rev Zairema suggested that the MNF might contest the then impending elections to the District Council, instead of going underground. Laldenga stated that his party was not yet strong enough to win the elections and that they were now not in a position to retreat from going underground.[13]

As a "self-respecting Mizo", Rev. Zairema could not bring himself to convey his conversations of December 1965 with Laldenga to the Government of India. Nevertheless, he pursued single-mindedly the idea of peace mission immediately upon the start of the MNF armed uprising. On March 12, 1966 the Standing Committee of the Presbyterian Church Synod held an emergency meeting, in which a representative of the Baptist Church of south Mizoram also participated. The meeting decided: a: to issue a public declaration and an appeal; and b: to constitute a Citizens Committee.[14] Thus, the important, perhaps crucial, role of the Church and the civil society behind the subsequent peace parleys had begun. Indeed, Church leaders like Rev. Zairema, Rev. Lalsawma, Rev. L. N. Ralte and Rev. H. S. Luaia representing both the Presbyterians and the Baptists, the largest Christian denominations in Mizoram, had taken a stand against violence from the very beginning and had also told Laldenga that the Church was against any attempt to seek help from China.[15]

The Public Declaration and Appeal issued by the Church amply demonstrated the views of the civil society in Mizoram for which the Church had in fact become the main rallying point. The Presbyterian Church issued a Pamphlet stating clearly that the Church condemned the violent activities in Mizoram, describing them as opposed to the teachings of the Gospel as also against the laws of human rights.[16] This was objected to by the *MNF Government*, which issued a counter order stipulating that those who violated any of their instructions would be brought to 'justice'.[17] At another meeting of the Standing Committee of Presbyterian Synod on 14 March 1966, it was decided to form a 'Christian Peace Committee' with members drawn from both the Presbyterian and Baptist Churches. This committee issued another pamphlet on 8-9 September 1966 essentially reiterating the Church's stand against violence and appealing for peace. For the first time, Rev. Zairema, Rev. L. N. Ralte and Rev. H. S. Luaia, representing the Peace Committee secretly met Laldenga at Sabual village on 2 November 1966 where they unequivocally condemned the letters sent by the MNF threatening the lives of many people and the forced collection of funds by masked MNF men at gun point. On the peace initiatives, however, no advance was made, perhaps, because of the presence of R. Zamawia, the MNF Defense Minister, who reproached H. S. Luaia and L. N. Ralte "for being anti-MNF and not neutral, and thus unfit to act as peace feelers".[18]

In March 1967, the Peace Committee met Sainghaka, the MNF Home Minister, and wrote to him in April that:

> "You have taken up this course in the firm believe that by doing so you will create better conditions for our children and the future generations to come. We admire the courage of your conviction. However, we would like to remind you that India herself has never been one nation. The Telugus are as different from the Punjabis as the Bengalis are from Mizos, yet we together are determined to build one mighty nation. In this process, each of us has a right as well as a responsibility, and the welfare of our children in future depends on how we discharge and exercise our respective rights and responsibilities. We would also like to point out that any self-respecting government should have naturally adopted the same attitude as the Government of India has adopted towards you. It might also be realized that the Government of India, in trying to keep up this self-respect and integrity, have incurred a great loss and a number of her sons too have sacrificed their lives. We firmly believe that the Government would go a step further to meet the desires of the Mizo people."[19]

They also urged Laldenga in May 1967 to allow the insurgents to avail of the amnesty offer made by the Government of India and advised him that such a gesture would open the possibility of negotiations.

The next move for talks was a secret meeting at Lengte village on 25 February 1969 arranged by Rev. Zairema and Rev. Lalsawma with C. Lalkhawliana, MNF Finance Minister, the only senior MNF official who had not yet taken shelter in East Pakistan by then. The meeting was set because B. C. Cariappa, the Commissioner of Cachar and Mizo Hills Division and the Central Government Liasion Officer, had earlier asked Rev. Zairema if the MNF would be ready for talks. Lalkhawliana gave them the following note: *"Knowing full well the stand of the Indian Government from the Church leaders, I am prepared to work and do my utmost to help create conditions that would lead to peaceful solution of the present situation provided, of course, the Government of India is prepared to respond to my appeal."* The Church leaders wrote to Cariappa in March, 1969 and attached the note from Lalkhawliana.[20]

Lalkhawliana on his part moved to East Pakistan with the copy of the note he had issued and the message he had received from B. C. Cariappa. Soon after his arrival in East Pakistan, an MNF Cabinet meeting was held at Rangamati on 17 April 1969, where he reported on his talks with the Church leaders. After a brief discussion, the Cabinet unanimously gave the MNF President, Laldenga full authority to explore the possibility of negotiations with the Indian authorities.[21]

As authorized by his Cabinet, Laldenga sent in late May 1969 Vanlalngaia, Director of MNF Intelligence Services and a ranking officer of the same directorate, Rozama, to meet B. C. Cariappa for making arrangements for negotiations. At the time he was deputed to make contacts with Indian authorities, Vanlalngaia inquired from Laldenga as to what was his concept of political settlement for Mizoram. Laldenga said, "The Kashmir parallel was already there. Settlement was made and Sheikh Abdullah was installed as Chief Minister." Vanlalngaia also insisted on a Cabinet authorization for his mission, which Laldenga had already obtained in April 1969.[22]

As B. C. Carriappa was away from his headquarters at Silchar, the MNF emissaries met M. V. Thomas, Assistant Joint Director of Subsidiary Intelligence Bureau, along with Rev. Zairema and Rev. Lalsawma at Lailapur Forest Rest House on 12 June 1969. The message that Vanlangaia and his colleague were to convey to Laldenga was not put in writing and was in the form of an "impression." The impressions they had are: 1. Any 'political settlement short of independence' could be discussed; 2. The venue for negotiations could be in a neighbouring country; and 3. In the mean time, the MNF forces should be allied with the Bengali freedom fighters in East Pakistan.[23]

Unfortunately, the Assam Police arrested the two emissaries near Karimganj on 15 June 1969 while on their way back to Dacca before they could convey to Laldenga the message they carried in their head.[24] As the news of their arrest and of the purpose of their mission came out in the press, Laldenga flatly denied any knowledge of their mission. At any rate, it could have been dangerous for him to own this up under the very noses of his Pakistani ISI minders. Instead, Laldenga deftly used this incident for maligning a group of the educated cadres who, he reckoned, had lost confidence in his leadership.

The MNF Split and Escape to the Arakan

He accused the group, sometimes referred to as 'Dumpawl' or Blue, of backtracking from their original goals. "I led you out of India; but I may not be fit to lead you back to it,"[25] he said to the guerilla commanders, implying that there were other leaders who were plotting to compromise with the Indian authorities. In March 1970, substantiating what was often described at the time in Mizoram as 'the split in the MNF,' he removed Lalnunmawia from the post of Vice President and installed S. Lianzuala in his place. He also removed his Army Chief, Sawmvela who was replaced by the MNF Defense Minister, R. Zamawia. The leading members of the so-called moderate group or the 'Blue' group, including

R. Zamawia this time, were arrested and put in prison in mid 1971 and were released on the eve of the MNF escape on 17 December 1971 from Bangladesh to Arakans in Myanmar. With the growth of Bengali freedom movement and with the future of East Pakistan becoming increasingly uncertain, Laldenga had become evidently eager to come to a political settlement with India. After Vanlalngaia's aborted mission, in 1970 and 1971 he sent at least 6 groups of emissaries to make secret contacts with Indian government.[26] Initially, he used for these errands an elite group of his personal guards called 'State Security Agents (SSA)' like Capt. Sangliana, Capt. Lalhleia, Capt. Thanthuama, Capt. Vaninmawia and Police SP Lalnghenga. The message they carried with them was: "If we have talks, we will be able to arrive at a peace settlement satisfactory to both parties." The standard reply from the Indian Intelligence was: "Government of India agrees to talks, provided the peace settlement is within the Indian Union." (R. Zamawia).

A group consisting of R. Liantluanga, MNF Deputy Commissioner of Bungkawn, Sailianpuia Sailo, an accounts officer and Lalruata, a ranking civilian official, seemed to have been taken seriously by the Indian authorities, perhaps, because they did not belong to Laldenga's personal staff. Except for the refusal by the Assam Chief Minister M. M. Chowdhury to meet them, (on the ground that he was "disgusted" at the duplicity of Laldenga), they met several high-ranking Intelligence and Army officials and were even taken to New Delhi. However, no real talks were arranged. This was in the months of June-July 1971. By then, New Delhi already had other plans, and talking 'peace' with Laldenga was apparently not one of its priorities. In fact, by December, with the creation of Bangladesh, Lalkhawliana, MNF Finance Minister, Lalhmingthanga, Foreign Minister, Thangkima, Education Minister, and 14 other high-ranking MNF personnel escaped from the MNF detention and came over to India to surrender. By now, several senior MNF cadres were available to help the Indian authorities glean the real intentions of Laldenga.

Since late 1970, India had been preoccupied with the 'liberation movement' in Bangladesh, which was expected to simultaneously deprive the MNF of safe sanctuaries and of active Pakistani assistance. The passing by the Parliament of the Northeast Areas (Reorganization) Act, 1971 also raised the political status of Mizoram to that of Union Territory, giving hopes of better political deal in future. At the birth of Bangladesh, the MNF movement was, perhaps, at its lowest point. After warding off the pursuing Mukhti Bahinis and Indian soldiers, Laldenga held a brief meeting of both civilian and army officers of the rank of Captains and Deputy Commissioners and above, where it was decided unanimously to depute one more mission to explore negotiations with the Indian government as also for all 335 non-combat civilians to return to Mizoram.

Lalnunmawia, former MNF Vice President and R. Zamawia, former Defence Minister, were appointed Special Envoys of the President and were also to escort the civilian group back to Mizoram. Their credential letter No. M-7/71/139 dated December 18, 1971 reads simply: "*The under-mentioned gentlemen are commissioned as Special Envoys of the President to act and speak on behalf of Government of Mizoram*" and was signed by Laldenga. Laldenga's parting words with Zamawia clearly showed his desperation. He said, "Try your utmost if only to save our lives."[27] They interacted once again with Indian intelligence officers. The initial responses they received from their interlocutors were like "things were different 8 months ago ... you are too late ...... don't expect anything big." The two emissaries returned with a message to the effect that "talks are possible" but without specifying 'when and where' were the talks should be held.

In the mean time, in February 1972 the Arakan MNF group was able to establish contact with the Pakistani Embassy in Rangoon. "Once Laldenga came to know that he would be able to travel safely to Karachi, he decided to cancel the mandate to negotiate he had given to us," said R. Zamawia. This was done by letter No. M-1/72/5 dated June 12, 1972 signed by S. Lianzuala, Vice President and Chairman, National Emergency Council (NEC). Laldenga and his family and close aides flew with travel documents under assumed names to Karachi in the third week of March 1972 and were lodged in the suburb of Rawalpindi.

Agreement of 1976

After the loss of East Pakistan, the Z. A. Bhutto Government had no use for Laldenga. "They reluctantly allowed him sanctuary in Rawalpindi out of a sense of obligation for his past deeds against India."[28] Laldenga's continued presence in Pakistan could have been an inconvenience at a time when its government was beginning to mend fences with India. His alienation from the Church leaders in Mizoram and his overtures to the communists in China and Burma had also taken away whatever credibility he may have otherwise had with the Christians and other altruistic organizations in the West and 'his opportunistic politics had shown through." [29] His efforts to find a sanctuary in Western countries had drawn blank. If he was going to be unwelcome in Pakistan before long, he seemed to have no option but to mend his fences with India. At any rate, reading from his past deeds, this seems to be what he had originally intended.

In November 1973, he sent his aides, Zoramthanga and Lalsangliana to contact the Indian mission in Kabul. This could not have been arranged without Pakistan's assistance, also implying that Pakistan was desirous of getting rid of Laldenga. Such a secret contact would be with the officers of the Research and Analysis Wing (RAW) in the Indian mission, who would pass on to New Delhi the news of their 'contact' with their comments and wait for instructions. Zoramthanga had to be sent again to Kabul nearly a year later, as no response seemed to be forthcoming from India. He must have adequately impressed upon the Indian intelligence operatives this time that Laldenga was sincere in his bid for peace and was ready to return to India when necessary. It was now arranged that he should fly to Geneva to meet a RAW officer, which he did on August 20 1974 on a passport issued by Pakistan in the name of Peter Lee.[30]

At Geneva, he met Hassan Walia, Additional Secretary, RAW and confirmed his willingness to return to India for talks by a letter to Prime Minister Indira Gandhi. The operative portions of the letter are:

"Since November 1973, my officials have been meeting your representatives ....I have already written to you...As I had mentioned, I have no doubt in my mind that the solution of the Mizoram political problem will have to be achieved within the Constitution of India....... In order that I could contact my underground colleagues for injecting into them my belief and conviction so that they come round to my line of thinking, I would request for the facility of my coming over to India.....For obvious reasons, I cannot tell them straight away that I have agreed to discuss the solution of the problem within the Constitution of India. Those people do not have the opportunity to appreciate the problem in the wider context of political developments all over the world."[31]

For the Government of India, however, it was crucial that Laldenga should come for negotiations only if he commanded the confidence of the rank and file of the MNF, which he did not appear to do, judging from his letter to Prime Minister Indira Gandhi. From this stage on, much input by the Indian intelligence agencies and the Mizo Church leaders had to be made into the processes through which a compromise of sorts was worked out within MNF leadership. As Laldenga had requested in his letter, New Delhi made arrangements in November 1975 for three of the top MNF leadership, Tlangchhuaka, the new MNF Vice President, Biakchhunga, Army Chief and K. Chawngzuala, MNF Party President, to join him in the talks he was having with Hassan Walia, the RAW officer. However, serious differences emerged between Laldenga and his colleagues, especially with Biakchhunga and Tlangchhuaka, during the nine days of discussions they spent in Cologne. It was decided that the three MNF leaders should proceed to New Delhi and that Laldenga would join them in the new year of 1976.[32]

Laldenga arrived in New Delhi on 24 January 1976 and soon he and his three colleagues went through five days of secret talks with Home Secretary S. L. Khurana, Mizoram Lieutenant Governor S. K. Chibber and Joint Secretary (Home) M. L. Kampani. On 18 February 1976, the MNF leaders and the Indian officials issued a signed 'Press Statement' in which the MNF leaders "acknowledged that Mizoram is an integral part of India and conveyed to the Government of India their decision to accept the settlement of the problem in Mizoram within the framework of the Constitution of India." The other passages of the statement were on the arrangements needed for the Calcutta MNF Convention to be held from 24 March to 1 April 1976 and for handing over of all MNF arms to the Central Government. The Convention was held at the "Meeting Hall" of SIB at Calcutta. The Indian Intelligence conducted the entire programme of the convention from behind the scene.[33] "Since the Raw-IB axis was organizing it all for the rebels, there seemed to be no hitches in the entire exercise."[34] At the Convention, the meeting was formally converted into an MNF Assembly and elected Laldenga as President and Tlangchhuaka as Vice President and elected Zoramthanga for the first time as General Secretary. It gave a mandate to the MNF delegation led by its President to negotiate peace settlement with India "within the Constitution of India." It also decided to convert MNF party into a legalized political party in India.[35]

After a "series of discussion" with the same three Indian officials, the following agreement was signed on July 1 1976 by Laldenga on the MNF side and S. L. Khurana on the government side.

1. "The MNF delegation acknowledged that Mizoram is an integral part of India and conveyed to the Government of India their resolve to accept a settlement of all problems in Mizoram within the Constitution of India.

2. In order to bring about a climate of understanding and an atmosphere of peace and tranquility in Mizoram at the earliest, the delegation agreed to abjure violence and suspend all activities. In furtherance of the above objectives, the underground delegation agreed to collect all underground personnel with their arms and ammunition inside mutually agreed camps within one month of their establishment and also agreed to hand over arms and ammunition to the Government of India.

3. The Government of India also decided to suspend all operations thereafter by the Security Forces. Such suspension, however, would not apply to operation against underground personnel attempting to cross international border and to the maintenance of law and order.

It was agreed to continue the talks further."

This understanding could not be implemented primarily because Laldenga could not fulfill his part of the deal. Doubts regarding the surrender of arms and certain opposition by some MNF leaders in Arakan continued. While the government insisted on the surrender of arms by the MNF should precede the political settlement, the MNF wanted it to be the other way round. Except for a brief interruption for the celebration of Christmas in December 1976, since October of that year, the Security Forces had already resumed operations, which had been suspended earlier in March. Peace talks also resumed but proceeded erratically.

Peace Talks and the Morarji Desai Government

In the general elections held in March 1977, the Janata Party came into power in Delhi. The new government resumed talks on May 18 with Laldenga to find ways to implement the July 1976 agreement signed by the previous government. Principled and rigid as Desai was, if he did anything, it was basically to alienate the rebels even more. The failure of these talks led the government to ask Laldeng to leave India by June 6, 1977. On June 9, a group of 62 MNF cadres, led by Sawmvela, ex-Chief of Army, surrendered their arms to the Lieutenant Governor of Mizoram and declared that it was immoral to continue the armed insurgency after the New Delhi accord of July, 1976.[36] Laldenga tried to appear reasonable by pleading for resumption of talks with the government, but he was again asked to leave the country by November 21. He somehow managed to stay on in Delhi and pursued further dialogue with the then Home Minister, Charan Singh.

However, these informal talks also broke down irretrievably in March 1978, because Laldenga refused to give up his demand for an interim government to be headed by him and his party colleagues. Even before the July 1976 agreement, he had repeatedly asked that a clause should be included whereby he should automatically head a provisional government before calling for fresh elections. His argument was that no real peace would come in Mizoram unless the terms of the agreement were implemented by both sides under his personal supervision. The government, however, had not accepted it. Perhaps, this was the reason why he had not made serious efforts to fulfill his obligation under the accord, despite the assistance of "RAW-IB axis" made available to him.[37]

Meanwhile in the Arakan Hills, in his absence, Laldenga was facing serious problems regarding the loyalty of some of the MNF leaders to him. A number of them were in no mood to follow his instructions blindly. Ignoring Laldenga, from June 1978 to April 1979, they even elected three different Presidents – Brig. General Biakchhunga (18 June – 26 October 1978), Tlangchhuaka (26 October 1978 – 24 January 1979) and Malsawma Colney (24 January – 11 March 1979). By this time, Zoramthanga, Secretary to Laldenga, and Major Tawnluia, ADC to Laldenga, had arrived from Delhi and, with the hardcore loyalists to Laldenga, they successfully plotted the arrest of Malsawma Colney and his followers on

11 March 1979. On 19 April 1979, they convened the MNF Assembly and elected Laldenga as President. Zoramthanga and Tawnluia became Vice President and Army Chief respectively, and those who had opposed the leadership of Laldenga were dismissed and allowed to return to Mizoram. Thus, the personal staff of Laldenga finally took over the MNF political organization, thereby providing him an 'unquestionable authority' to negotiate with the Indian Government.[38]

In Mizoram, Brig. T. Sailo and his People's Conference Party won the elections in May 1978 and formed the new government. As he was allied with Janata Party, which had dismissed the peace talks with Laldenga as meaningless, Sailo's detractors accused him of being an obstacle to peace talks. They also blamed his 'advice' for the arrest by New Delhi of Laldenga on 8 July 1979.[39]

Return of Congress (I) to Power & Politics of 'Peace Talks'

Indira Gandhi returned to head the government in New Delhi in January 1980. The leaders of the Congress Party in Mizoram lost no time in pleading to her to resume talks with Laldenga. Laldenga was released from prison and all charges against him were withdrawn on 30 June 1980. Counter-insurgency operations in Mizoram were also suspended. Laldenga first had talks with Home Minister Giani Jail Singh before the veteran diplomat, G. Parthasarathy, then Chairman, Policy Planning Division, Ministry of External Affairs, was entrusted with the task of negotiating peace settlement with Laldenga. But the talks were doomed to fail again as the 26-point proposals made by the 'MNF Executive Committee' included some demands, which the government regarded as totally unacceptable. Parthasarathy could have perhaps whittled down Laldenga's demands to two essential points - to elevate Mizoram to a full-fledged State and to make Laldenga the Chief Minister of the interim government. Full statehood for Mizoram had already been agreed to in principle, but removal from Chief Ministership of Brig. T.

Sailo would have been constitutionally impossible, as he refused to vacate his office and insisted on a contest in an election.

In Mizoram, hardly anyone believed any more, by then, that peace could come without prior assurance to Laldenga that he would head the interim administration following the peace settlement. And people knew that the vital piece for the rebel leader was still missing in the MNF-Government settlement arranged so far. They also knew that in the absence of settlement the MNF would resort to renewed violence and that the response to such a renewed violence by the government would be massive. By a notification dated 20 January 1982, the government again banned the MNF. Laldenga was asked to leave the country and he left for London on 21 April 1982. By the middle of 1982, 26 battalions of various units of Security Forces were operating in the State.[40] With several rounds of cease-fire and suspension of operations since the first peace parley, people had become used to a relaxed tenor of life. The new restrictions on movement and dust-to-dawn curfews were a bitter reminder of the early days of the MNF insurgency and had a great psychological impact on the people. Demand for peace and agreement with the government begun to proliferate. The Baptist and the Presbyterian churches had always stood firm for peace. They were now joined by the powerful students union (Mizo Zirlai Pawl), opposition MLAs and leading members of the civil society. Very soon, for the politicians, clamour for peace talks became a powerful means of rallying support and an effective weapon against the Sailo government and his People's Conference party, who were held responsible for the failure of the MNF-Government talks and the current suffering of the people.

The People's Conference Party (PC), once considered sympathetic by the MNF, now became a target of covert and overt threats of attack by the latter essentially because of Sailo's attitude towards peace settlement especially his refusal to step aside to give way for Laldenga.[41] The order issued on 10 August 1982 by MNF Vice President Zoramthanga, in fact, included order to assassinate several PC leaders.[42] The PC was thus no longer safe for surrendering MNF cadres to join. The Congress Party led by Lal Thanhawla decided to campaign for the ouster of the Sailo government on a platform of peace. The Congress Party attracted many ex-MNF cadres who felt safe being in it, which was now seen as the best bet for bringing about the next peace talks. The underground elements of the MNF also were using selective violence in support of the Congress. The Congress Party in Mizoram had been informally in contact with Laldenga after the break down of the talks in 1982. They had been consulting with the central Congress leadership in Delhi as to how Laldenga should be dealt with. Finally from London, Laldenga decided to support the Congress in the elections due to be held in April 1984. Thanhawla had sent two emissaries to meet Laldenga in London, who managed to bring taped speeches of Laldenga in support of the Congress in Mizoram. One of the emissaries, Lalduhoma, who had resigned from the Indian Police Service to join the Congress, was "planted by Laldenga" (R. Lalawia) to ensure that the Mizoram Congress did not renege on its commitment to renew the peace talks.[43] With this background of preparations, the Congress Party won the 1984 Assembly elections easily, and on 5 May 1984, Lal Thanhawla became Chief Minister.

The Final Accord with Laldenga

On 6 September 1984, Laldenga issued a statement in London that he was ready to issue 'orders' to his followers for an immediate ceasefire as a first step to a negotiated settlement of the Mizoram problem. He returned to Delhi on 29 October 1984. He said, "I have come back as an Indian to solve our problem and take my place as an Indian in Indian politics".[44] The talks got going immediately. Unfortunately, Indira Gandhi was assassinated on 31 October 1984. Laldenga had in fact been scheduled to meet her at 5 o'clock on that evening. And the central government became preoccupied with the problems of law and order following the riots given rise to by the assassination of Indira Gandhi.

Laldenga had to wait for a few months. On 15 February 1985, Laldenga met the new Prime Minister Rajiv Gandhi. The negotiations were now entrusted with Home Secretary R. D. Pradhan. The talks could not be concluded in 1985. Laldenga left for London on 24 December ostensibly to celebrate Christmas with his family. On 27 February 1986, an all-party meeting in Mizoram along with the Students Action Committee issued a joint call for all concerned to solve the insurgency problem once for all. They also submitted a memorandum to the Prime Minister urging resumption of the peace talks.

On 15 June 1986, Laldenga returned to New Delhi to resume talks. As the result of intra-Congress Party consultations, an arrangement was devised for the Mizoram Chief Minister Lal Thanhawla to resign to make way for Laldenga. A 'Confidential' Agreement between the MNF Party and Congress Party was thus signed on 25 June 1986 by Laldenga and Arjun Singh, Vice President of the Indian National Congress. The crux of this accord was that it stipulated in its first article: "*On a date agreed to between Shri Laldenga and the Government of India, Shri Lal Thanhawla, the present Congress (I) Chief Minister will submit his resignation and Shri Laldenga will be elected the leader of the Government of Mizoram and be sworn in as the Chief Minister there.*"[45] Finally, Laldenga was about to realize his longstanding and cherished ambition. The Peace Accord, technically titled, "Memorandum of Settlement," was signed on 30 June 1986.[46]

Main Factors Behind the Accord

There were three main factors interacting in the process of the peace negotiations. A brief recap and an appraisal of the roles played by these elements may help in determining the clinching factor.

1. *Laldenga and the MNF:* Laldenga was keen to arrive at an early solution, but it must be one in which he would be able to call the shots in Mizoram following the settlement. This insistence was of course due to his political ambition;

it could also be to ensure safety for his life as he was said to be extremely distrustful of others concerning his personal safety and position.[47] However, he needed time to convert to his "line of thinking" the fighting cadres, largely composed of ex-servicemen and uneducated and hot-blooded young men, who blindly believed in the 'struggle for independence'. This change of course could have been accomplished sooner than it was, had he taken the educated leaders into confidence. Perhaps, there was the danger of being labeled a fraud and ousted by another artful leader. However, the knowledge by the Government since July 1969 that Laldenga was ever ready to negotiate was an essential input into the process of peace negotiations.

2. *The Establishment:* This consisted of the Congress (I) government at the Centre and the local administrations in Mizoram. Most of the leading *'over ground' political leaders* of then Mizoram were deeply saddened by the tragic turn of events that the MNF movement had triggered. *The Mizo Union leader* such as Ch. Chhunga and his colleagues were evidently willing to make necessary sacrifices for peace, but there was nothing that they could do to initiate peace moves as the 'MNF government' was bent on paralyzing their authorities. In April 1971, for instance, they offered in writing to concede to the MNF 75 % of the legislative seats in the elections expected to be held upon the elevation of Mizo Hills to the status of Union Territory in early 1972.[48] But by then Laldenga was busy sorting out his alleged detractors within the MNF leadership. Ch. Chhunga also resigned in May 1977 from the Chief Ministership, hoping this would facilitate settlement with the MNF.[49] As *Brig. T. Sailo and PC Party* took a principled stand and rejected the idea of making Laldenga the Chief Minister in the interim, they were accused of sabotaging the peace talks in 1982 and they were virtually "at war" with the MNF.[50]

The contribution of the *Mizoram Congress (I)* under the leadership of *Lal Thanhawla* toward the peace settlement was difficult to differentiate from the efforts of the central leadership of the party. Much credit has been given to the integrative vision espoused by Indira Gandhi towards the separatists in the Northeast and her efforts to penetrate ethnic insularities and extend participative democracy by devolution of appropriate autonomies.[51] (Amidst the multiple ethnic communities in the Northeast, as the government must have realized by now, devolution of power on the basis of ethnic identities has at times led to fragmentation and tendency towards ethnic radicalism with violent consequences.) And this overall approach was said to be at the background of the Centre's handling of the Mizo problem. This strategy of 'peace making' also certainly carried with it the policy of projecting the Congress (I) as the defender of the cause of peace in Mizoram, which indeed helped it to consolidate its mass support there. It is in the execution of this policy that Lal Thanhawla performed creditably. The fact that he was ready to vacate his office to make way for Laldenga was also creditable, but then, given the scheme of Indira Gandhi's strategy, a refusal could also have cost him his leadership.[52]

3. *The Civil Society:* Much has been written about the role of the civil society and the Churches in this paper. With their impeccable credentials as workers for the advancement of the society and their prestige as religious leaders, the Church leaders were fearless and naturally became the spokesmen for the civil society and the common people at large. They were firm in their conviction that the MNF had forced Mizo people to take a wrong turn.[53]

As for the common people, with the break down of yet another peace talk in the early 80s, they had become literally "fed up" with the insurgency. They simply wished to be left alone to live their own lives. All they wanted was peace at any price. At any rate, the overwhelming majority of the Mizos had never been taken in by Laldenga's propaganda, in the first place. The Mizo Union, the largest political party then, was solidly against the idea of rebellion and, as the result, a number of its activist were victimized and killed by the MNF soon after the outbreak of the insurgency. Apprehensive of the disastrous consequences a rebellion could bring to the people, many educated Mizos openly countered and even ridiculed the MNF propaganda.[54] Once the real intention of Laldenga became publicly evident, the people clearly sensed the futility of prolonging the insurgency. It could thus be safely asserted that upon the assumption of power by the Congress (I) in early 1984, most Mizos simply expected the new State government to be fully engrossed in peace making and in ending the insurgency. In other words, insurgency was no longer 'feasible' as a political strategy in Mizoram. It had to be ended by whatever means available. Fortunately for the remaining MNF cadres, the common people were now largely ready to forgive and forget. In the ultimate analysis, therefore, it was the will of the people that ended the insurgency.

By the same token, it is the will of this same people, which has sustained peace in Mizoram so far. This is, in spite of the inadequate and improper fulfillment by the government of the clauses in the Peace Accord concerning the rehabilitation of the reformed rebels and relief of the victimized innocents during the insurgency.[55] These (Article 13.) were the only provisions that could have gone some way in healing the "wounds," no matter how differently the victims felt. Two decades have now passed after the Mizoram Peace Accord was concluded. How long the people will be prepared to continue to preserve peace will depend largely on the performance of those gentlemen, who are managing the affairs of the people on the pretext of governing them.

APPENDIX - 1

CONFIDENTIAL

Agreement Between the Indian National Congress (I) and the Mizo National Front, Mizoram

The Government of India under the leadership of Shri Rajiv Gandhi has brought about a situation wherein the long years of disturbed conditions in Mizoram are being brought to an end. The Memorandum of Settlement is being signed between the Government of India and Shri Laldenga, President of Mizo National Front, to give shape to this effort to usher peace and prosperity in Mizoram within the framework of the Indian Constitution. Shri Laldenga has pledged to bring the MNF into the mainstream of the Indian polity and irrevocably commit it to strive for a strong and united India.

In order to further strengthen this resolve and to enable a smooth and orderly transition, the Indian National Congress (I) and the MNF headed by Shri Laldenga agree to form a coalition Government. This decision shall be implemented soon after the members of the MNF, who are underground, lay down their arms and join the national mainstream.

1. On a date agreed to between Shri Laldenga and the Government of India, Shri Lal Thanhawla, the present Congress (I) Chief Minister will submit his resignation and Shri Laldenga will be elected the leader of the Government of Mizoram and be sworn in as the Chief Mnisiter there.

2. Shri Lal Thanhawla, the present Chief Minister, shall be sworn in as the Deputy Chief Minister.

3. In addition to the Deputy Chief Minister, four members of the Congress (I) Party shall be made Ministers of the new Government.

4. In addition to the Chief Minister, three members of the MNF Party will be made Ministers.

5. The names of the Ministers will be nominated by the respective Political Parties and the Chief Minister will propose them to the Lieutenant Governor.

6. All issues concerning the formation and induction of this new Government will be decided mutually by the Chief Minister and the Deputy Chief Minister.

7. In order to smoothen the function of the coalition Government, a coordination committee will be constituted consisting of the following:-

a. Shri Laldenga, Chairman, b. Shri Lal Thanhawla, Vice Chairman, c. Two members of the Congress Party; d. Two members of the MNF Party.

This committee will take into consideration all matters concerning the Party and the Government, which either of the Political Parties may deem necessary to bring for its consideration in order to help smooth functioning of the Government and to bring better coordination between the Congress (I) and MNF.

8. This coalition Government will continue to function till such date when the President is satisfied that normalcy has returned and the holding of elections has become feasible.

9. In the event any difference arising between the two parties, they would seek the help of the Hon'ble Prime Minister.

Sd/-Laldenga
President
Mizo National Front.

Sd/-Arjun Singh
Vice President
Indian National Congress
2nd June 1986.

APPENDIX - 2

MIZORAM ACCORD (1986)

Memorandum of Settlement

Preamble

1. Government of India have all along been making earnest effort to bring about an end to the disturbed condition in Mizoram and to restore peace and harmony.

2. Toward this end, initiative was taken by the late Prime Minister Shrimati Indira Gandhi on the acceptance by Shri Laldenga on behalf of the Mizo National Front (MNF) of the two conditions, namely,cessation of violence by MNF and to hold talks within the framework of the Constitution. Aseries of discussions were held with Shri Laldenga. Settlement on various issues reached during the course of the talks is incorporated in the following paragraphs.

Restoration of Normalcy

With a view to restoring peace and normalcy in Mizoram, the MNF Party, on their part, undertakes within the agreed time-frame to take all necessary steps to end all underground activities, to bring out all underground personnel of the MNF with their arms, ammunition and equipment to ensure their return to civil life, to abjure violence generally to help in the process of restoration of normalcy. The modalities of bringing out all underground personnel and the deposit of arms, ammunition and equipment will be worked out. The implementation of the foregoing will be under the supervision of the Central Government.

The MNF Party will take immediate steps to amend its Articles of Association so as to make them conform to the provision of law.

The Central Government will take steps for the resettlement and rehabilitation of underground MNF personnel coming over ground after considering the schemes proposed in this regard by the Government of Mizoram.

The MNF undertakes not to extend any support to the Tripura / Tibal National Volunteers (TNV), Peoples Liberation Army of Manipur (PLA) and any other such groups, by way of training, supply of arms or providing protection or any other manner.

Legal, Administrative and Other Steps

4.1 With a view to satisfying the desires and aspirations of all sections of the people of Mizoram, the Government will initiate measures to confer statehood on the Union Territory of Mizoram, subject to the other stipulations contained in this Memorandum of Settlement.

4.2 Togive effet to the above, the necessary legislative and administrative measures will be undertaken including those for the enactment of Bills for the amendmentsof the Constitution and other laws for the conferment of Statehood as aforesaid, to come into effect on a date to be notified by the Central Government.

4.3 The amendments aforesaid shall provide, among other things, for the following:

(1) The territory of Mizoram shall consist of the territory specified in Section 6 of the North Eastern Areas (Reorganisation) Act, 1971.

(2) Notwithstanding anything contained in the Constitution, no Act of Parliament in respect of:

(a)Religious or social practices the Mizos, (b) Mizo customary law or procedure, (c) Administration of civil and criminal justice involving decisions according to Mizo customary law, and (d) Ownership of property and transfer of land, - shall apply to the State of Mizoram unless the Legislative Assembly of Mizoram by a rsolution so decides.

Provided that nothing in this clause shall apply to any Central Act in force in Mizoram immediately before the appointed day.

(3) Article 170 Clause (1) shall, in relation to the Legislative Assembly of

Mizoram, have effect as if for the word 'sixty' the word 'forty' has been subsitued.

5. Soon after the Bill for conferment of Statehood becomes law, and when the President is satisfied that normalcy has returned and that conditions conducive to the holding of free and fair elections exist, the process for holding elections will be initiated.

6. (a) The Centre will transfer resources to the new Government in view of the change in status for a Union Territory to the State and this will include resources to cover the revenue gap for the year.

   (b)Central assistance for Plan will be fixed taking note of any residuary gap in resources so as to sustain the approved Plan outlay and the pattern of assistance will be as in the case of special category States.

7. Border trade in locally produced or grown agricultural commodities could be allowed under a scheme to be formulated by the Central Government, subject to international arrangement with neighbouring countires.

8. The Inner Line Regulations, as now in force in Mizoram, will not be amended or repealed without consulting the State Government.

Other Matters

9. The rights and privileges of the minorities in Mizoram as envisaged in the Constitution shall continue to be preserved and protected and their social and economic advancement shall be ensured.

10. Steps will be taken by the Government of Mizoram at the earliest to review and codify the existing customs, practices, laws or other usages relating to the matter specified in clauses (a) to (d) of para 4.3 (2) of the memorandum, keeping in view that an individual Mizo may prefer to be governed by Acts of Parliament dealing with such matters and which are of genral application.

11. The question of unification of Mizo inhabited areas of other States to form one administrative unit was raised by the MNF delegation. It was pointed out to them, on behalf of the Government of India, that Article 3 of the Constitution of India prescribes the procedure in this regard but that the Government cannot make any commitment in this respect.

12. It was also pointed out on behalf of the Government that as soon as Mizoram becomes a State:

    (i) The provisions Part XVII of the Constitution will apply and the State will be at liberty to adopt any one or more of the languages in use in the State as the language to be used for all or for any of the official purposes of the State.

    (ii) It is open to the State to move for the establishment of a separate Univeristy in the State in accordance with the prescribed procedure.

    (iii) In the light of the Prime Minister's statement at the joint conference of Chief Justices, Chief Ministers and Law Ministers held at New Delhi on 31st August 1985, Mizoram will be entitled to have a High Court of its own, it it so wishes.

13. (a) It was noted that there is already a scheme in force for payment of ex-gratia amounts to heirs/dependents of persons who were killed during disturbances in 1966 and thereafter in the Union Territory of Mizoram. Arrangements will be mad e to expeditiously disburse payments to those eligible persons who had already applied but who had not been made such payments so far.

    (b) It was noted that consequent on verification done by a joint team of officers, the Government of India had already made arrangements for payment of compensation in respect of damages to crops, buildings destroyed/damaged during the action in Mizoram, and rental charges of buildings and lands occupied by the Security Forces. There may, however, be some claims, which were preferred and verified by the above team but not yet settled. These pending claims will be settled expeditiously. Arrangements will also be made for payment of pending claims rental charges of land/building occupied by the Security Forces.

Sd/- Laldenga On behalf of Mizo National Front.	Sd/- R.D. Pradhan Home Secretary Government of India	Sd/- Lalkhama Chief Secretary. Government of Mizoram

Dated: 30th June, 1986
Place: New Delhi.

REFERENCES

1. For instance, R. Zamawia believed that the "struggle for independence for Mizoram was assigned to him by God." R. Zamawia, former Defense Minister, MNF at an interview on 18. 11. 2005.
2. Quoted by James Dokhuma in Ch. Chhunga Chanchin (Biography) and reconfirmed by C. Pahlira in an interview on 20. 11. 2005.
3. C. Pahlira, *Ibid.*
4. Verghese, C. G. & Thanzawna, R. L. A History of the Mizos, Vol. II, pp. 79. "One of these authors," without identifying which one, claimed to have been told by an ex-MNF official that the latter had collected Rs. 40,000 from Chaliha in 1963 for passing on to Laldenga.
5. Verghese, C. G. and Thanzawna, Ibid. Vol. II pp. 22. The visit was arranged by R. Zamawia through the then Assistant High Commissioner of Pakistan, Shillong.
6. Sajal Nag, Contesting Marginality , 2002, pp. 218, quoted by C. Nunthara in a seminar paper 'Analysing the Mizo Peace Accord'.
7. Tawrhbawm Daily of 12. 6. 2003 and confirmed on 22. 11. 2005 in an interview by R. Lalawia, former Speaker of Mizoram Assembly (1999 - 2003), who also said that Laldenga had discussed the same point with him on two occasions.

8. Witnessed and reported by Denghnuna, IAS (retd), then District Information Officer, Mizo Hills.
9. The portion on the meetings on 28 February 1966 is from an interview with R. Zamawi held on 18. 11. 2005.
10. Verghese, C. G. & Thanzawna, R. L., pp. 77, *Ibid.*
11. C. Lakhawliana, MNF Finance Minister, at interview on 22. 11. 2005.
12. C. Lalkhawliana, MNF Finance Minister, *Ibid.*
13. Rev. Zairema, then i/c Presbyterian Mission in Cachar District, at an interview on 22. 11. 2005. Rev. Zairema told me that he had not revealed this conversation with Laldenga to anyone intending to put it on record. He now wanted that "the truth be told."
14. John Vanlal Hluna, Quoted by J. S. Jafa, in Mizoram: Contours of Non-military Intervention, Faultlines
15. John Vanlal Hluna, *Church and Political Upheaval in Mizoram,* (Aizawl, Mizo History Association, 1985), pp. 111-121.
16. Declaration and Appeal of the Church - dated 12. 3. 1966 quoted by John Vanlal Hluna, Ibid.
17. MNF Home Minisry's Letter dated 16. 3. 1966. Quoted by John Vanlal Hluna, *Ibid*
18. R. Zamawia, *Ibid.* and John Vanlal Hluna, *Ibid.*
19. R. N. Prasad, *Government and Politics in Mizoram,* pp. 209-210, quoted by V. S. Java, *Ibid.*
20. Rev, Zairema, *Ibid.* and c. Lakhawliana, *Ibid.*
21. C. Lalkhawlian, Ibid. This should also put to rest the allegations often made against Laldenga by ex-MNF cadres that he made peace overtures without consulting the MNF leadership.
22. Vanlalngaia at an interview on 20. 11. 2005. He said that his mission was decided over a glass of beer at a restaurant in Dacca Inter-Continental Hotel. According to him, Laldenga opened up after he showed Laldenga a letter he had received from E. L. Mendus, a former Christian Missionary in Mizoram, who had advised him that he and his politician friends would be able to organize assistance for Mizoram if the MNF could arrive at a political settlement within the Indian Union.

23. Vanlalngaia, *Ibid.*
24. Nirmal Nibedon, Mizoram: The Dagger Brigade, Lancers Publishers, New Delhi, 1980. pp. 146.
25. Vanlalngaia quoted by Nirmal Nibedon, *Ibid.* pp. 145.
26. R. Zamawia, then MNF Defence Minister and Army Chief, Ibid. These are with his personal knowledge. He believes that there were more messengers deputed to India.
27. R. Zamawia's Manuscript.
28. V. S. Jafa, *Ibid.*
29. Bualhranga, MNF Senator at an interview on 26. 11. 2005.
30. Nirmal Nibedon, *Ibid.* pp. 208.
31. M. C. Lalrinthanga, Mizoram Politik Aizawl, 1993, pp. 4 & Biakchhunga, former MNF Army Chief, Hnam Kalsiam, Aizawl, 1996, pp. 97-98
32. Biakchhunga requested Laldenga to return to Arakan to sort out the issue with National Council but the later refused. Interview with Biakchhunga on 15. 11. 2005.
33. M. C. Lalrinthanga. *Ibid.* pp. 17.
34. Nirmal Nibedon, *Ibid.* pp. 211. 'Rebels' here means Laldenga and his confidantes such as Zoramthanga, the present Chief Minister, Tawnluia, Home Minister and a few others. Most of the participants in the Convention did not have idea of why the whole tamasha was done this way.
35. M. C. Lalrinthanga, *Ibid.* pp. 18.
36. V. S. Jafa, *Ibid.* The sequence of events in this section is largely taken from his paper.
37. Nirmal Nibedon, *Ibid.* pp. 211.
38. M. C. Lalrinthanga, *Ibid.* pp. 97-103. Lalrinthanga later visited Delhi and personally reported the news of the successful plot to Laldenga on 1 May 1979.
39. M. C. Lalrinthanga, Ibid. pp. 109. He quoted then Home Minister H. M. Patel' statement on 10. 7. 1979 in the Lokh Sabha, "As proposed by the Mizoram Chief Minister, Laldenga was arrested."

40. V. S. Jafa, *Ibid.*
41. M. C. Lalrinthanga, Ibid. pp. 138. He said that PM told Laldenga that the Sailo government did not belong to her party and therefore she could not ask them to step down.
42. Quoted in full by M. C. Lalrinthanga, *Ibid.* pp. 151-154
43. R. Lalawia, *Ibid.* He claimed that he had given a rent free house for five years and a hundred thousand Rupees to Lalduhoma so that he could be politically active and work for peace. Lalduhoma became the President of the Congress and MP eventully. He did leave the Congress later and joined the MNF Party.
44. Ved Marwah, Uncivil Wars, Harper Collins, 1995, New Delhi. p. 266.
45. The Text of the Agreement is at Appendix 1.
46. The Text of the Peace Accord is at Appendix 2.
47. R. Zamawia, *Ibid.*
48. V. Laichhinga, MNF Deputy Foreign Secretary, at an interview on 24. 11. 2005. He was deputed to urge the Mizo Union leaders not to accept the Union Territory status in April, 1971 but was told by Ch. Chhunga that it was too late to change the situation. Instead, the Mizo Union leaders made the proposal in writing. V. Laichhinga was arrested on his return to the MNF Hqrs. But he handed over the papers he was carrying to the arresting officers.
49. Animesh Ray, *Ibid.* p. 176.
50. M. C. Lalrinthanga, *Ibid.* p. 154.
51. V. S. Jafa, *Ibid.* and Ved Maewah, *Ibid.* p. 269.
52. According to Lal Thanhawla's brother-in-law, R. Vanneia, the former had offered to vacate his office during the pre-election campaigns leading to the 1984 MLA elections. No record is available on this. On the other hand, soon after the take over of power by Lal Thanhawla, the then Congres (I) President , Lalduhoma complained in a letter to Lalsawma, that the ruling party was trying to avoid taking steps towards 'peace talks'. In protest, he resigned , and formed another party called 'Mizoram Peace Congress;.

53. Rev. L. N. Ralte wrote on 7 March 1966 in a Visitor's Book of a Rest House he had fled to at the outbreak of the insurgency, "I prayed that the Indian forces may annihilate the MNF." Rev. H.S. Luaia and Rev. C.L. Hminga drove to Aizawl to plead to the District Commissioer T.S.Gill and the Army Commanders not to burn villages on the way to Lunglei. They on their part persuaded the MNF not to attack the oncoming Security Forces. As the result, Lunglei was spared the straffing and bombing that Aizawl had suffered. Rev. H. S. Luaia also gave a tip to the possible location of an arms cache hidden by MNF. (R. Zamawia, Ibid.)

54. A veteran politician who at one time was Minister in the Assam Government, A. Thanglura commented that fighting for independence was like trying to dive into a flat rock. He was also quoted to have said, "If the MNF attain independence, I offer myself to be slaughtered for the celebration." These quotations were spread all over Mizoram.

55. Prof. Lianzela, Paper "Mizoram Peace Accord" presented at the OKD Institute of Social Change and Development, Guwahati, in February 2005.

5

OF PEACE AND DEVELOPMENT IN MIZORAM: A PERSPECTIVE

I am thankful to the OKD Institute of Social Change and Development for providing me with the chance to share some thoughts about the current situation in Mizoram. I particularly appreciate this opportunity of making the acquaintance of fellow Northeasterners, who are knowledgeable about the numerous problems vexing our region. I am sure that this Workshop will be a landmark in my learning process. And that, in fact, is the reason I dared accept the invitation to participate, even though, I knew, I do not possess the competence to do so.

A truism that has often been used to explain the lack of development in a region affected by armed conflicts of one kind or another is: peace and development are indivisible and where there is no peace, there can be no development. *The reasoning is that there is a logical link between peace and development.*

The Mizos, especially the politicians, are fond of proclaiming that Mizoram is the most peaceful State in the Northeast. Ever since the signing of the Mizoram Accord or "Memorandum of Settlement" between the Mizo National Front (MNF) and the Government of India on 30 June 1986, the State has indeed been largely free of armed conflicts. There have been occasional but minor incidents of armed activities perpetrated, mostly in the border areas, by underground groups based from outside the state such as the Chin National Army (CNA) from Myanmar, Zomi Revolutionary Army (ZRA) from Manipur, Bru National

Liberation Force (BNLF) from Tripura and Hmar People's Convention-Democratic (HPC-D) from Assam and Manipur. However, these incursions have neither been serious nor frequent enough to disrupt the process of development work. By the logic of 'development linked with peace', Mizoram should thus have advanced ahead of most of the Northeast States still troubled by insurgency.

However, even to a casual visitor to the countryside, it becomes obvious that Mizoram has a long distance to cover in the path of the eradication of poverty, not to speak of achieving prosperity. Let us take just the situation in the energy supply, a crucial infrastructure sector which, in Saddam Hussein's parlance, must be described as "mother of all sectors of development." The current position regarding the supply and consumption of electricity is: Estimate of requirement - 120 MW as against existing supply of 72 MW; electricity generated by the State: 22 MW (Diesel: 16 MW and Mini/Micro: 6 MW); purchased from neighbouring States: 50 MW[1] . A State that is 50 MW short of its energy requirement is unlikely to be able to make much headway in development. Other sectors of infrastructure do not seem to fare better either. Whether it is in human resource development, public health services or transport system, Mizoram faces a daunting task of quality up-gradation.

With a record of nearly two decades of peaceful political climate, why is Mizoram still at this stage of development? Why didn't it acquire a status, worthy of emulation by other States of the NE? Or is there something wrong with the kind of peace Mizoram has attained? What are the reasons behind this reality? These are some of the questions I will presently attempt to address in this paper.

Peace Accord

A quick look at the Peace Accord and its background is perhaps appropriate, as the Accord was supposed to have triggered the development process. The earliest peace overture made by the MNF on record was the dispatch of two ranking intelligence officers to make contact with the Indian authorities in mid-1969, about three years after the start of the insurgency. The move apparently made on his own by the MNF President, Laldenga, came to be known by his cabinet colleagues only when the two officers were arrested by the Indian Army on July 5, 1969 at Karimganj, Assam.[2] [3] Next came his by now famous letter written on August 20, 1975 to Prime Minister Indira Gandhi.[4] The letter clearly indicates that there had been regular contacts between the Indian authorities and the emissaries of the MNF since late 1973. The crucial importance of the letter, of course, is that it clearly spelled out: 1) that the MNF chief was agreeable to seek solution to the Mizo problem within the Constitution of India; 2) that his senior colleagues had not been informed of this and would need to be persuaded; and 3) that he required the assistance of the Indian authorities to persuade them.

Apart from whatever motives the MNF leader might have had on his own for initiating peace process at that stage, the pressure of public opinion, overwhelmingly in favour of peace, spearheaded by the Church, political parties especially the Indian National Congress and NGOs would have been difficult to ignore. As the result of his unilateral initiative, he had little or no bargaining leverage in the peace talks. The ensuing protracted peace parleys and the reasons why the Peace Accord took so long to be concluded are beyond the scope of this paper. Considering the horrible sufferings that the insurgency and the counter-operations by the security forces brought on innocent people, these are still fitting topics for a thorough research.

As for the Accord, except for providing to cover the "revenue gap" of the state for 1986-87, it does not contain any provisions that could significantly accelerate the process of development. (No details of the Accord are given here as another paper has been written on the subject). The Memorandum of Settlement is essentially concerned with the conferment of statehood to Mizoram and the attendant legal and administrative questions. Even the status of statehood, according to the first Chief Minister of the Union Territory of Mizoram, the late Ch. Chhunga, was "available" for the asking in 1971, the year in which North Eastern Areas (Reorganisation) Act was passed and a decision to confer statehood to Meghalaya and Tripura was arrived at. He said, "Since our underground brothers would have nothing but a statehood to bring home eventually, we left it for them to bring it home. We had thus to be content with the status of Union Territory"[5] The statement could have perhaps been an exaggerated interpretation of the apparent willingness of the government of India then to accommodate the demand for statehood, provided that would lead to the end of insurgency in Mizoram. At any rate, the peace of mind that the cessation of insurgency brought to the people appeared to be enough of a bonus by itself.

Government of India's Attitude

The actual provisions of the Peace Accord notwithstanding, the central government had clearly intended to help develop Mizoram as a model state in the Northeast, once peace could be somehow put in place there. The objective was to demonstrate that "peace pays" by helping the newly peaceful Mizoram generate development to the extent that it would become worthy example for other insurgent groups, a catalyst for peace, as it were, in the whole region. "Let there be cessation of insurgency first, then we shall see the rest," so the argument went.[6] The actions taken by the central government immediately upon the conclusion of the Accord amply demonstrated this attitude.

Just a week after the signing of the Accord, Prime Minister Rajiv Gandhi and family, Sonia Gandhi, Pryanka and Rahul, visited Mizoram for four days from 9 to 12 July 1986, an unusually long and intimate visit by a head of government to a tiny state like Mizoram. The PM personally drove to the southern, eastern and northern fringes of Mizoram. He also convened on 11 July a meeting of all Chief Ministers of the Northeast States and Union Territories in

Aizawl to assess the impact of the Mizoram accord and consider measures to curb insurgency in the region. And at the end of the visit, he declared that, if peace held, he would turn Mizoram into 'a land of milk and honey'.

Then, in early August 1986, a team of eight central Ministers, accompanied by concerned senior officials in their respective ministries, headed by N. D. Tiwari, Minister of External Affairs, came to Aizawl with the express purpose of helping Mizoram to formulate a master plan for development. The team apparently found the Mizoram government unprepared for meaningful interaction, perhaps, because it was still in transition from a status of Union Territory to full statehood. "They were surprised at the visit and were totally at a loss as to what to suggest to such a powerful team," was how one participant from Delhi put it.[7] [8] After sanctioning a few pending project proposals, the central team had to return to Delhi without carrying back with them any far reaching ideas about the development of Mizoram.

Development in the Post-Accord Mizoram

What is even more surprising is that the interim UT government as also the following state government did not subsequently take up the Centre on its original (obvious but not written) 'promise' of transforming Mizoram into a model state. Instead, they turned legalistic and clamoured for "full and speedy implementation" of the Accord, which, as made clear already, had no provisions of significant import for economic development. One allegedly 'unimplemented' clause of the accord (3.3) relates to the rehabilitation of the 600 odd MNF returnees. The central government initially sanctioned Rs. 15 crores for this, which apparently did not reach properly all the intended beneficiaries.[7] The other provision of the accord that causes controversy is concerning indemnities to be paid to the heirs/dependents of persons who were killed or whose properties were destroyed during and following the 1966 'disturbances'. The initiative needed for the closure of this issue is also clearly dependent on the state government. Important though these matters might have been for the affected individuals and for the 'healing process' of the trauma of the insurgency, they are not vital factors for development.

An example of the present state of development in Mizoram, i.e. the situation on energy supply, has been mentioned earlier. Seen with the wisdom of hindsight in the context of the Center's plan to make Mizoram a model of development, it is clearly the failure of successive ministries after the Accord that is to blame for the current dismal state of affairs in Mizoram. An exception perhaps was Brig. T. Sailo's ministry, which was in power in 1979-1984, well before the peace accord was signed. The first and, one must say, the only systematic plans for building infrastructure, especially in the transport and power sectors, were formulated and begun by that ministry. However, most of these projects have remained unimplemented today. The most glaring example among them is the 120 MW[8] Bairabi Hydro-power Project on the Dhaleshwari (Tlawng) river for which Detail Project Report was completed way back in 1984.

One is not concerned here with assigning blames on the various ministries for their evident failure to take advantage of the 'generosity' of the central government then. Nor would it serve any purpose to lament over their failure. It is to establish that, in the absence of a competent agency to generate development, peace *per se* does not/cannot produce any meaningful development. 'The longer peace lasts, giving time to those in charge to make a mess, the more intractable the problems become' - seems to be what Mizoram today has signified. It may, therefore, be pertinent to conduct a brief survey of conditions in Mizoram today[12] in order to surmise: what a failure to make a purposeful use of peace can bring to the lot of a people in the NE and what this may portend for their future.

As noted earlier, Mizoram is critically deficient in infrastructure building. Take the example of Bairabi Thermal

Power Plant with a capacity to produce 22MW of electricity, which was set up at a cost of Rs. 105 crores and was inaugurated early this year. It is now lying idle, not for want of fuel as claimed by the authorities, but because the estimated unit cost is too high to be introduced to public consumers.[9] Around Rs. 9 crores of compensation has recently been awarded for land and properties to be affected by a 12MW Hydel Project at Tuirial, making it almost certain that this mini project will also become cost-ineffective.9 The post-Accord governments have not been able to produce even one cost-effective infrastructure project so far.

The unsystematic approach to infrastructure development has now resulted cumulatively in the distortion of the whole development process. Added to this is rampant corruption rooted in the nexus of politicians and officialdom. In such a situation as this, no sector of the economy can be expected to produce any significant progress. Agriculture, the mainstay of rural economy, has remained stagnant. The bulk of essential items of food continue to come from outside the state. Private sector is unable to take off, thereby failing to play its important role of generating jobs. Instead, government service becomes the main stable source of employment, leading to surplus staffing of the government. The income gap between urban and rural dwellers is steadily widening. The rate of growth of educated unemployed is rapid, now stated to total close to one lakh, in a population of less than one million. With in-patients in the main Civil Hospital requiring to have their lab tests at private laboratories and having to pay for syringes and bandages, the health care system cannot afford much care. Critical drinking water problem in dry season continues unabated. There continues a decline in per capita success rate of young graduates in the national level competitions for jobs owing to lack of quality education. A random illustration of the economic situation, such as is given here, is perhaps enough to show that the development process is in a state of an alarming disarray.

Faced with a dismal prospect on all fronts, the general public has become very pessimistic and negative in its attitude towards the government. As not many expect the authorities to help them improve their ways of eking out a living, they would rather stake a share directly on the 'development monies' by whatever means available to them. In other words, corruption begets corruption. The system has become so corrupt that the only way to be able to benefit from it is to become corrupt oneself. This is not about a simple corrupt practice, packed with perks and fringe benefits, which still produces the intended results, though at a bloated cost. It is about a system, which can no longer steadfastly pursue its avowed objectives - a system perhaps heading towards a collapse.

Thus, threats and pressures have become the most effective means of extracting group interests and concessions from the government. NGOs like the Church, the Young Mizo Association (YMA) and the Mizo Zirlai Pawl (MZP–Mizo Students' Union) have become unduly influential not only in the discourse of policy issues but also of routine administrative matters. Then, there are numerous professional unions, who have often held the government a virtual hostage when they felt that the latter infringed on their 'legitimate' interests.

An instance of the immobility of the government in the face of public arbitrary conduct is sharply focused in the current yearlong campaign launched by the YMA against drug abuse and drug smuggling all over the state. The YMA campaigners are often reported to have openly destroyed the houses and properties of "proven" (not by law court) drug dealers. A group called "MTV" even claimed to have maimed several of them. This crusade is increasingly assuming a classic case of mob rule. The authorities have yet to insist that these campaigns should be conducted in accord with the rule of law. It is at present left to NGOs like the Human Rights and Law Network and some enlightened individuals to try and limit their excesses.

One can cite numerous cases of the manifestation of social tensions and despondent anxieties arising from the perception of the common people that the authorities, present or past, are not really fit to eventually improve matters. What has been briefly pointed out in the foregoing should be sufficient to give a glimpse of Mizoram after two decades of the signing of the peace accord.

Beneath its peaceful picture so often proudly painted by its complacent politicians, Mizoram is fraught with problems, which they are not about to solve. For how long the place will remain as peaceful as it has been in the last so many years is anybody's guess. One thing seems certain. That is that if the common people in Mizoram ever again decide to have a violent revolt from sheer frustrations, it may not be against the Centre. Most likely, it will be against the misrule of their fellow Mizos.

NOTES & REFERENCES

1. *Midterm Appraisal of the Tenth 5-Year Plan, Planning Board, Government of Mizoram, 2004.*
2. Biakchhunga, Hnam Kalsiam - Nation Building (Mizo) - pp.92. See lso End Notes -i.
3. Copy of the letter is at Annexure.
4. Statement made on 24.2.1987 at a meeting to celebrate Mizoram State at the residence of Ch.Chunga and quoted by B. Zaliana in his book : '*Mizoram Political Parties - Documentary Records*' pp 42 (Mizo).
5. See End Note - ii
6. Dr. J. V. Hluna, Head of History Department, Pachhunga University College, Aizawl.

   See also End Note-iii.
7. Animesh Ray, *MIZORAM*, National Book Trust - pp. 210. See also End Note -iv
8. This was reduced in 1999 to 80 MW in order to avoid multiplying compensation claims and to make it cost effective.
9. A Source in the Power and Electricity Department.

ANNEXURE
HOTEL, du LAC

Rotissene Box
COPPET
R. COTTRAUX. MAITRE. ROTISSEUR
TELEPHONE (D22) 761521
TELEX 27639 : CABLE : HOTLAC.

To,

The Prime Minister,
Govt. Of India
New Delhi

Dear Madam Prime Minister,

Since November 1973, my officials have been meeting your representatives to discuss the question of restoration of peace and normalcy in Mizoram for an ultimate settlement of Political problem. In pursuance of these discussions. I have already written to you a letter mentioning therein about my willingness to discuss the solution of the problem within the Constitution of India. Your officer wanted to meet me personally and so at grave personal risk I have managed to come out of Pakistan and met your representative Mr. Singhal at Geneva. I had lengthy discussions with him regarding the various implications of the problem following this. I am writing this personal letter to you with the fervent hope that it will meet your kind consideration.

As I had already mentioned, I have no doubt in my mind that the solution of the Mizoram Political problem will have to be achieved within the Constitution of India. While therefore I can assure you that there would be no constitutional problem in finding out the desired settlement, I would like to put forth that our social, cultural and religious traditions and customs would necessitate some special safeguard. For this purpose, some minor administrative adjustment would have to be found during the Political talks.

In order that I could contact my underground colleagues for injecting into them my belief and convictions so that they come round to my line of thinking. I would request for the facility of my coming over to India, which I am prepared to do. As I will have to take the greatest risk in coming out of Pakistan once again which will be for good, I would need this assurance from your goodself. I also hope that your Government would grant us suitable safe conduct while in India and extend facilities to contact my underground colleagues which may be at places convenient to you. The underground leaders whom I like to meet first are my Vice President Mr. Tlangchhuaka, MNF Party President Mr. Chawnzuala, my Army Chief Mr Biakchhunga and Col. Zamana. Given the opportunity to meet and discuss with them the various aspect of the problem, I am confident and can assure you that I would succeed in bringing them over to my line of thinking for a settlement of the problem.

For obvious reasons I cannot tell them straight away that I have agreed to discuss the solution of the problem within the Constitution of India. These people do not have the opportunity to appreciate the problem in the wider context of Political developments all over the world. I would therefore have to explain to them all these in details and give them some hope. I am unilaterally issuing instructions to my colleagues to refrain from operation so that a conducive atmosphere as desired by your representative could be created in the field before and during the talks. A copy of my letter is enclosed for your information. I do hope that your kind self may like to consider issuing some secret instruction to your armed forces in Mizoram for reciprocal action. I could then assure my colleagues that I had requested the Govt. of India for cessation of hostilities.

I hope the above mentioned points will receive your kind consideration and that all these correspondence of mine will be treated with utmost secrecy. Your Govt. representative Mr. Singhal has however assured me about it. Only if strict secrecy is maintained about my correspondence to you, I would be able to convince my colleagues without the feeling that I am working under any duress.

Profound regards,

Yours sincerely,

Sd/- (LALDENGA)

20.8.75

6

INDIA'S LOOK EAST POLICY: A PERSPECTIVE*

I feel flattered to be invited to speak to a gathering of distinguished professional economists. It would, however, be foolish on my part to behave as an economist and begin talking about economics. All I can do here appears to be to tell a story, which has some tedious connection with economic. It is about how India's Look East policy came about.

As a follow up of a joint Australian-South Korean proposal mooted a year previously, in late 1989, Economic Ministers of 12 Pacific rim countries met at Canberra and proposed to constitute themselves in what was tentatively called 'Asia Pacific Economic Cooperation (APEC) Grouping'. The group was formally set up as APEC at a meeting of Heads of Government and the representatives of 19 countries at Blake Island in the US in 1993.

The 1989 Canberra proposal then aroused a keen interest in some development economists and immediately attracted attention of the world wide economic media. Some quarters, however, including the government of India[1] initially dismissed it as an US design to wield its economic influence in the Pacific region. However, we in the Indian Embassy in South Korea inquired into how exactly this proposal was initiated. It transpired that the joint proposal had been

---

* Seminar paper on The Look East Policy. Venue: Itanagar, Arunachal Pradesh. June 12, 2008.

made during a visit by the Australian Prime Minister to South Korea in early 1989. The Indian Embassy was convinced that the proposed grouping was a serious initiative for long term regional economic cooperation. We also learnt that, except for the insistence of the Japanese, the initiators of the idea, the South Koreans and the Australians, had not even included the US in their original list of proposed participants. We therefore reported our finding and proposed to our government that India should bid for an active association with the group right from the time when its organizational structure and objectives were still being processed.

Our proposal was initially rejected as being hasty, especially when the proposed group had not yet defined its objectives and format. However, a chorus of support by the Indian Ambassadors in the region helped convince eventually the government of India to authorize us to formally submit our request for participation in the proposed group in whatever status the members of the group themselves deem fit. Along with this, we also proposed that India should seek partnership with the ASEAN, the Association of South-East Asian Nations, which had then clearly demonstrated the advantages of regional economic cooperation.

India is now a dialogue partner with ASEAN and is engaged with its members in various cooperative economic activities, while it has been participating in several activities of APEC, including the important Security Summits held at regular intervals.

During the consultations in the course of the considerations of the above two proposals, much correspondence and interlocution took place between New Delhi and its representatives deployed abroad in the southeast and northeast Asian regions. What emerged from this exercise was a firm conviction that while India should continue to maintain close cooperation with the West and other regions like Africa and Latin America, it should pay much more serious attention to its relations, particularly with regard to economic cooperation, with the countries in its immediate eastern neighborhood and beyond. Upon the formation of the Narasimha Rao government in Delhi in 1991, our present Prime Minister, Manmohan Singh as Finance Minister steered India's economic policy towards a steady liberalization of various state controls. And this eventually led to an official stamp of approval of 'the look east initiatives'.

The so-called 'Look East Policy' of India is thus not so much of a policy as an ongoing process of a series of initiatives for broadening and deepening our economic and other cooperation with the countries in the dynamic growth regions of southeast and northeast Asia. As far as I know, there is no White Paper on it. It can also be described as a creative attitude towards global cooperation as distinct from a specific and a formal policy. Indeed, such an attitude would have evolved, at any rate, in the thinking of any keen observers of global development trends even in the early days of globalization.

Since the government of India announced its 'look east' intentions and commenced taking initiatives in this direction in the early 90s, bilateral trade exchanges with some of the countries in the regions have not only grown exponentially, but there has also been a rapid increase in bilateral, sub-regional and regional linkages and institutional interactions, aimed at enhancing and consolidating all round cooperation.

I was fortunate to be again associated personally with this process while serving as Indian Ambassador in Myanmar in the years 1995 and 1996 and as Indian Trade Representative in Taiwan during 1997-2000. From Myanmar, we made several proposals for cooperation. Most important among these proposals were: Joint venture for hydro-power project on the Chindwin river; Reintroduaction Indian Airlines flight from Kolkata to Rangoon, which had been suspended for over 20 years; Joint exploitation of Myanmar's gas deposits in Arrakan; Multi-modal project for development of Highway,

Inland Waterway on Kalodyne, Sittwe Port and Hydro-power generation from a dam on Kalodyne; Railways to link Myanmar via Jiribam - Imphal valley through to Kalewa (Tahan) in Myanmar; Highway to be constructed by India from Champhai to Falam in Myanmar; Reconstruction of the Stillwell or old Burma Road from Assam via north Myanmar to Yunnan in China, etcetera. Some of these proposals have been taken up and some are still being pursued. The highway project linking Moreh in Manipur to Kalewa in Myanmar was also sanctioned during our tenure in Rangoon. So was the bridge across the Tiau river to Rih as also Border Trade Posts at Moreh-Tamu while border trade posts at Champhai-Rih was under consideration. Our main preoccupation in Taiwan was with trade and investment promotion.

In order to demonstrate the current dynamics of India's proactive attitude in this direction, we may cite just a few examples:

1. In 1992, UN's Economic and Social Commission for Asia & Pacific regions (ESCAP) based in Bangkok endorsed the Asian Land Transport Infrastructure Development (ALTID). Thereafter, it revived the Asian Highway (AH) and the Trans-Asian Railway (TAR) projects, which had been held in abeyance since 1959 and 1960 respectively. Inter-governmental agreements were concluded - for AH on November 18, 2003 and for TAR on July 4, 2004.

2. Agreement on Bangladesh - India - Myanmar - Singapore - Thailand Economic Cooperation (BIMSTEC) was established in 1997. Its principal aims are eventual free trade, investments, tourism and technical cooperation.

3. Kunming Initiatives (1999) – a meeting of non-official think tank group as well as businessmen was convened at Kunming, the capital of Yunnan province, China, to explore ways for sub-regional economic and cultural cooperation. Representatives from Bangladesh, China,

India and Myanmar (BCIM) participated and the group now called 'BCIM Economic Cooperation Forum' has been meeting at various locations in one of the 4 countries every year. The main objective of this group is to generate ideas and device mechanisms for sub-regional cooperation extending over Southwest China, Myanmar, Bangladesh and Northeast India.[2]

4. Free Trade Agreements with Thailand, Singapore Indonesia and Brunei by 2011 and with Philippines, Cambodia, Laos, Myanmar and Vietnam by 2016.

5. Mekong-Ganga Cooperation, etc.

6. There are a number of cooperation agreements at bilateral level too. For instance, an Indo-Myanmar bilateral agreement of far-reaching significance to Northeast is the Multi-Modal Inland Waterway-cum-Highway project on the Kalodyne River, estimated to cost $ 104 million. Under this project, Sittwe Harbour in Rakhyne, Myanmar and navigation on Kalodyne as also Highway from south Mizoram will be developed so that Northeast is directly linked to a seaport. All the attendant protocols to the agreement have been signed and the project is ready to take off.

Look East Policy & Northeast

India can hardly look 'eastward' without also looking at the Northeast region! As indicated earlier, the 'Look East Policy' is part of India's response to the process of globalization. In other words, NE region will largely have to participate in the ongoing process of globalization by means of the series of initiatives India and its eastern partners take for expanding mutual cooperation spanning over and through the NE region itself. One certain thing to be noted is that we cannot avoid or escape from this inexorable process of globalization. Nor will it be wise to try and resist or oppose globalization, for the NE is too insignificant a region to influence this massive international game. India has decided to be an active participant in this game and all we need to do, therefore, is to prepare for the challenges we must face.

The process of globalization obviously has several aspects; and some new elements may yet emerge as it is navigated and steered into 'exotically' backward economic sub-regions like the Northeast India's. However, there appear to be at least three ingredients which inevitably accompany the process of globalization wherever it spreads. These are: it is technology driven; it is privatization centric; and it is opposed to market barriers or its effectiveness and its benefits to the participants thereof depend largely on open and free market. These are some of the elements of globalization, which we have to reckon while pondering over the hard challenges we may have to face, once the Northeast is effectively exposed to its processes.

Based on what can be discerned from the various interactions and linkages proposed so far, we can visualize a rough sketch of the NE scenario as follows:

1. Apart from the much needed upgrade of infrastructure, e.g. power generation, there will be a greatly enhanced connectivity comprising land, waterways and air.
2. This will entail much more open borders than the existing situation, and will inevitably lead to massive movements of people both domestic and across borders. The theme of this seminar, "Northeast as a Common Market" will truly happen then.
3. An explosion of tourism can be expected to accompany these.

These are only brief illustrations of what can happen and of how our region will be transformed. As none of the State Governments in the region appears to be well aware of the process of globalization and India's look east initiatives, let alone be ready for them, the civil society as well as academia will have to play an active role in anticipating and assessing, and preparing for, the likely impact of this global process on our communities.

REFERENCES

1. Note prepared for PMO and circulated in late 1989 or early 1990 by M. Dubey, Secretary (Economic Relations) and later Foreign Secretary in MEA.

2. The writer is also a member since 2005.

7

CONNECTIVITY AND NORTHEAST: IS THE NORTHEAST READY?

Background

Although several regional and sub-regional linkages have been proposed for India's Northeast (NER), the region has continued to remain poorly connected. Apart from the opening in April 1995 of the Tamu - Moreh border trade posts on the Indo-Myanmar border and the recent elevation of the Guwahati Airport to an international entry point, there has not been any significant progress in the proposed linkages. Along the Indo-Bangladesh border, the existing authorized border trade posts are: in Assam – Dhubri, Sutarkhandi, Gokalganj and Mankacher, in Meghalaya – Dawki, Bholaganj, Shella Bazar, Balat, Borsora, Dalu and Mahendraganj, and in Tripura – Akhaura, Simanthapur and Rajan. Compared to the pre-Independence land and waterways connectivity available for the Northeast, the existing channels of trade and transport routes are far from adequate to have any opening impact on the over all insularity of the region.

This imposed insularity, as it were, on these historically isolated ethnic societies has over the years given rise to a whole range of attitudes, which have transformed into a mindset, peculiar to the various ethnic groups of the region. What is often termed as the 'alienation' of these communities from mainstream India is also mainly due to this physical isolation. There is this vague sense of "we" as distinct from "other Indians", which some observers even tried to conceptualize as 'nationalism or sub-nationalism' (Sanjib

Baruah et al). Whatever this is, by cutting off its traditional market access and main transport routes, the partition did cause a serious set back to the economies of the region, of which proper assessment has yet to be made.[1]

The so-called indifference of the Centre, as at times alleged by some local lobbies, to the development of the region does not appear to be the primary reason for this 'alienation'. After all, the per capita funding for development in NER, particularly in the small States of the hill areas, has remained far above the national average.[2] The strategy embedded in *India's Look East* policy of providing a thorough going connectivity to NER, therefore, stands the best chance of bringing about, in the long term, a *total solution* to the various problems affecting the NER today.

However, the moot question to be asked is: are the communities and the institutions in NER ready for creation of such connectivity? There appears to be a few issues that need to be addressed by both the central and the state governments before a wholesale construction of the major projects for the connectivity can be embarked upon. This note is thus an attempt to highlight in a power point fashion some of these issues, with a particular focus on Mizoram, whose problems are also largely common with the other NE states.

Present Scenario

1. The proposed *Asian Highway (AH)* network and the *Trans-Asian Railway (TAR)* systems do not touch the two least connected States of NER, Mizoram and Tripura in India and also Chin State in Myanmar.

2. The envisaged super East-West highway within India is also said to terminate at Silchar, Assam, without reaching Manipur, Mizoram or Tripura.

3. The civil society in Mizoram is much exercised about these. On its part, it recently suggested inclusion of an AH diversion linking Agartala - Aizawl (in India)-

Tiddim or Falam - Kaleymeo (in Myanmar). It also proposed a highway link from south Mizoram to Dhaka - Yangon highway project, which now seems at a standstill. (NER Vision-2020 prepared by North Eastern Council (NEC).[3]

4. With the government of Bangladesh opting out of the AH system, however, even if the governments of India and Myanmar agree to take up the proposal, the prospect for its approval at the multilateral level is now dim.

5. The proposed AH diversion from Sylhet - Karimganj - Silchar (Assam) - Jiribam - Imphal (Manipur) - Tamu (Myanmar) also now seems meaningless.

6. If reconstruction of Stilwel Road is not taken up, AH will thus be confined to the existing road from Guwahati to Tamu via Assam, Nagaland and Manipur, without providing any additional international connection to NER.

7. Thus, Bangladesh is the key to NER connectivity and development. There is of course *mutuality of multifaceted interests in this sub-regional interdependence, which India's diplomatic practice would no doubt take into account as it appears to have done in the relations with Myanmar.*

8. India is also engaged in upgrading Rhi - Tiddim and Rhi- Falam roads in Myanmar.

9. The other proposed trade route through Champhai (in Mizoram) - Rhi on the Indo-Myanmar border has yet to be inaugurated.

10. Along the 310 km. long Indo-Bangladesh border shared by Mizoram, there has not been any authorized border trade post so far. Mizoram recently proposed opening of one such at Demagiri across Kaptai Dam in Bangladesh.

11. The Multi-Modal Highway-cum-Inland Water Transport project on the Kaladan river in south Mizoram is yet to be taken up.

Some Impediments to Connectivity

1. The problem of *illegal immigration* continues to be a sensitive issue throughout NER. Even a relatively ethnically pure and geographically isolated society like that of Mizoram is vexed by this problem. Further connectivity is bound to compound the problem.

3. The *inadequate awareness* by the political leaderships, the bureaucracies and civil societies in NER states of the ramifications of India's liberalized policies and, for that matter, about the long term implications of the Look East policy for the region is another loophole. Reform process has hardly begun. There is no trend towards privatization and no real attempts are made to promote the role of the private sector in development. The current attitude of the common people is that the government is responsible for handing out development. No rational plans for attracting *FDI / domestic investors* are in place.

4. This attitude towards development and the 'mindset' referred to earlier prevent people, including NGOs, from perceiving development issues in the larger national perspectives. For instance, the proposed GAIL/ONGC gas pipeline from Myanmar that is expected to pass through Mizoram is being vehemently opposed by the Chakmas and some NGOs, for they do not regard the project as directly beneficial for them while they stand to lose large tracts of farm land.[4] Projects of national import can at times be vulnerable to a sabotage by a few ill-informed 'indigenous' populations.

5. The existing *infrastructure* especially the power and services sectors are not enough to support creation of the envisaged connectivity. Take the example of energy supply, except perhaps for Arunachal, the power situations in the other states are not nearly enough to take advantage of the envisaged enhanced connectivity of the region. Even if highways and railways pass through the region, the common people will just be bypassed and they will not

have the capability to make use of the new opportunities brought about by the connectivity.

6. There is the regime of blocking out interaction between NER people and foreigners, known as *Restricted Areas Permit for foreigners*. Under this system, no foreigner, even if he/she has a valid visa for entry to India, can visit much of the areas of the NER hills, without first obtaining an RAP from the Home Ministry of India or the Home department of the state concerned. No Indian missions abroad are authorized to issue this permit to visit the specified areas in NER without the clearance of the Home Ministry. Promotion of *tourism* for the region, for example, seems meaningless.
7. There is also a regulation called *Inner Line Pass (ILP)* regime, which prohibits all outsiders including Indians citizens not belonging to the states from visiting Arunachal, Mizoram and Nagland unless they have a valid *ILP*, issued by the state governments for a specified duration.
8. The *land holding system* which prohibits non-domicile entities from acquiring real estate is another hindrance. In Mizoram, even owning of businesses by outsiders is banned.
9. *Security problems* continue to infest NER. Insurgency or rather the practice of insurgency or lawlessness has become a thriving business in some parts of NER. Except for the Naga insurgents, most of them do not fight for real political causes. "These are nothing but organized mafias"[5] (K. Kipgen). Politicians are often alleged to abet their activities, especially during elections.

Some Suggestions

1. **Work permit** regime for foreigners may provide an effective solution to immigration concerns. At any rate, a proper system for the regulation and record of the movements of people across borders need to be put in place by the states concerned.

2. **Improved border management** appears to be overdue. Opening of *international entry/exit points* at Tamu-Moreh and Champhai-Rhi could be considered or preparations could commence.

3. **Restricted Areas Permit** regulation for foreigners must be withdrawn, in order to promote tourism and exposure to the youth.

4. **Inner Line Pass** system within the same country is an absurdity, but it has been there for long and the people feel safe from the "danger" of being swamped by outsiders. The civil society will need some persuading before it can be removed. No state government, of its own accord, is likely to change it unless it is pressed by the people.

5. **A paradigm shift**, every study reckoned, is required in the approach to the development of the region. It could be in the form of a *participative planning and implementation* whereby the civil society is directly involved in the planning stage, monitoring and evaluation of execution of projects, as is being attempted by the recently reconstituted NEC. Development funding could also be made conditional on the direct participation of the stake holders. The *Northeast Study Group* constituted by the Home Ministry recently submitted to the government an insightful and detailed reports and recommendations on a 'new paradigm for the development of NER' including a *strategy for dealing with insurgency* there. The concerned authorities in the Centre and the States could pursue the recommended guidelines of the Group.

6. At any rate, insurgency cannot be eliminated without active aid of the populace. The *Mizoram experience* clearly showed that civil society could render insurgency 'irrelevant' as a political strategy.

And, above all, a *culturally friendly mode of partnership* with the civil society, especially the stakeholders, must be developed while 'navigating and steering' the process of globalization into the region. Along with this, *cultural highways* across borders in the region could be opened to enable exchanges of cultural troupes, sportspersons, students, etc.

For creating partnerships with the civil societies, NEC is perhaps the most suitable to take initiatives through NGOs, concerned and knowledgeable in NER. The meetings of BCIM Forum, or of its sector groups, if any, could also be held some times in the region in cities with facilities like Guwahati or Shillong. NEC could also be involved by funding and organizing such meetings.

CONNECTIVITY & INVESTMENTS

Impacts and Implications

The primary component of India's Look East Policy is to provide Connectivity and its attendant inflow of investments, both FDI and domestic, to the Northeast Region (NER). In other words, the idea is to transform NER into a linkage corridor between India and its immediate neighborhood of Myanmar and beyond. It really means Globalization of NER, no less. (The issues raised in the following are illustrative and are only meant to kick-start a discussion.)

A properly connected NER will be, among others:

- Its transport systems, *road, rail, air and waterways,* will have been integrated into the currently envisaged network of transport linkages between India and South-east Asia/South-west China, such as the proposed Trans-Asia Railways (TAR), Asian Highway systems (AH), etc.
- Become an integral part of the networks of broad banded information highways and of other modes of communication world-wide.
- Much more relaxed than the existing entry regimes will have been put in place along the Indo-Bangladesh

and Indo-Myanmar borders, with easy access to transit routes.

- Such a connected NER will also have acquired essential support of infrastructure, particularly, adequate supply of power and efficient and reliable services sectors.
- NER then, with its mild climate, will have become an attractive place for investments for high-tech industries, especially for those with products normally transported by air and requiring air-conditioning facilities. It will become suitable location for plants that manufacture goods for export to China and Southeast Asia as well as for those that work on the natural resources of NER and Myanmar.
- A rapid expansion in tourism industry is bound to accompany this.
- The technologists and the trained personnel required for servicing such an expansion in investments and services sectors will have to be, at least at the start, from outside the region.

Are our *communities* and *institutions ready* for such a pervasive permeation/infiltration, with its inevitable consequence of intercultural interactions? With a focus largely on Mizoram, the obvious points for consideration are:

- Our land holding system, with the regime of restriction on holding by nonresident non-Mizos.
- The RAP and ILP regimes, with the continuation of which globalization of the place is near impossible.
- The ban on owning of businesses by outsiders and the restrictive regime on *behnami* businesses.
- Are our NGOs such as the Churches, YMA, MZP, etc. ready? Can they be less 'xenophobic' overnight than they currently appear to be?

- Can we, i.e., the state governments, protect businesses and businessmen / tourists from insurgents or those groups who thrive on the practice of insurgency?
- Are our young men and women fit and competent to mix freely with affluent 'outsiders' in the work places and socially?
- Is the MLTP Act (total prohibition) a hindrance to our connectivity?
- After all, are we psychologically prepared to open up and be part of the global market?

Regrettably the answer is No. We are not at present yet ready for a thorough going connectivity. We need to change for our own good. I believe, we can change and adjust to the necessities of the market. For this, we need a political set up that is aware of the problems and requirements ahead of us.

REFERENCES

1. B. G. Verghese reckons it to be "at least a quarter century" back, (India's Northeast-Resurgent).
2. Against the national average of Rs. 1,080, Arunachal received central assistance of Rs, 36,237 while Mizoram and Nagaland received Rs. 23,177 and 32,567 respectively as far back as the 8th Plan period. (Gulshan Sachdeva, *Economy of the Northeast,* 2000)
3. Report prepared by Centre for Northeast Studies & Policy Research, New Delhi, Mizoram Chapter, 2005
4. The original proposal mooted when the writer was Indian Ambassador to Myanmar was to bring the pipe along the Kaladan river and generate thermal power in Mizoram for distribution though the existing network of national power grid.
5. K. Kipgen, IAS (Rtd) former Chief Secretary & Advisor to Governmor, Manipur, Report of Northeast Study Group of Home Ministry, 2004.

8

WHAT PRICE FOR PEACE?*

The government claims that the present decision is intended only to widen ceasefire area, without any commitment whatsoever to alter existing State borders. This still begs the question why it took the risk of provoking unrest outside Nagaland at this stage. Why pursue this negotiating strategy? THE RECENT Central Government's decision to apply its ceasefire agreement with NSCN(I-M) to areas of Manipur and Assam "inhabited by Nagas," betrays a certain shortsightedness, if not ignorance, about the ground realities of Northeast (NE) politics. For non-Nagas in the surrounding areas of Nagaland, the message implicated by the decision is immediately clear peace with the Naga insurgents at any cost. How else would they have read the `writing on the wall'? "Ceasefire" with the Naga rebels has been extended to their own `homesteads', over the heads of their home-grown insurgents, whose numbers and disruptive capacities are considerable, if not equal to that of the NSCN's. How is this going to help them attain peace in their areas?

At the same time, for the NSCN stalwart, Thungaleng Muivah, a Tangkhul Naga from Manipur, this decision could be counted as one of his crowning achievements in the longish history of his insurgent existence. For, it is no mean feat, even for a hardcore rebel like Muivah, to have

* *The Hindu,* Online edition of India's National Newspaper, Tuesday, July 24, 2001.

been able to pull off an "annexation", albeit by way of "ceasefire," of virtually two- third of Manipur to his cherished dream of "greater" homeland for the Nagas. That too, not by sword but by "diplomacy". This is the stuff of brilliance in negotiation rarely surpassed even by the best of our diplomatic brains abroad.

The Less Useful Galf

Our man or men in Bangkok and those in North Block who have been mulling over their briefs might argue that the NSCN, in both its (Muivah) and (Kaplang) incarnations, is the wellspring of insurgencies in the Northeast; that it has been the main trainer of other insurgents in the region and a facilitator of arms supply to them, either by way of purchases, rent or grant; that, therefore, once ceasefire is secured and peace is put in place with the Naga rebels, it may follow with the rest, and so on. This is at best half of the truth and the less useful half at that.

The other half of the truth is that there have long been genuinely autonomous insurgency movements in both Assam and Manipur. The United Liberation Front of Asom (ULFA) and the People's Liberation Army (PLA) of Manipur, particularly, have been hustling and, at times and places of their choice, hurling havoc at our security forces for years. Of the numerous "banned" insurgent outfits in the NE, most of which are specific tribe- oriented (such as Hmar People's Conference (HPC), Kuki National Army (KNA), Zomi Revolutionary Army (ZRA), etc.), these two insurgent groups, ULFA and PLA, can be said to have acquired the capacity to force a level of `accommodation' with the local authorities. The ease and the confidence with which they collect funds and "taxes" even from high officials and politicians and the extent of influence they wield on overground politics are the unmistakable evidence. At least, these two groups need to be reckoned with, for any meaningful ceasefire' to be effective in Assam and Manipur, parts of which are now "covered" by the ceasefire agreed with the NSCN(I-M).

The Real Issue

The real issue at stake, at any rate, as is seen in Manipur, is not about ceasing fire; it is about the five-decade-old demand by Naga rebels of all factions for the integration of the "Naga occupied areas" into Nagaland. This will involve incorporation into Nagaland of most of three districts of Manipur, namely Ukhrul, Senapati and Tamenglon, and a large chunk of North Cachar Hills district of Assam. Of course, the non-Naga inhabitants of Assam and Manipur, whether located `underground or above ground', vehemently oppose this. Thus, the inclusion of these areas in the ceasefire arranged with Muivah and his associates cannot but be seen by them as a ploy to find a way to accommodate the insurgents' demand.

Given the sensitive ramifications and the intractability of the issue, any conclusive discussion on matters pertaining to outside the borders of the present Nagaland should have been kept as one of the last items of the agenda at the Bangkok talks. The fact that NSCN's claim of "vital connectivity" to outside Nagaland had now been discussed, though for a seemingly innocuous purpose of securing a wider ceasefire area, gives rise to several complex issues. The attitudes of non-Nagas affected by the claim are likely to harden. It has given a common cause to oppose to rebels and non-rebels alike in the affected areas, particularly in Manipur. If the ceasefire idea is pursued, the collective fury it provoked at Imphal recently may turn out to be a starter only. Any non-Naga politician in Manipur seen to be acquiescing in any concessions made in the present talks will now be extremely vulnerable.

Indeed, it has raised a new political issue in the NE, that is, the issue of the permanence or otherwise of the existing arrangements of borders amongst the NE States, which are mostly of mixed ethnic populations. Questions such as these are bound to be asked: If the Nagas of Manipur are added to Nagaland, what about the Mizos of southern Manipur, bordering Mizoram and so on? What will Manipur be like, then? Among others, this is likely to generate a new and popular anti-Delhi movement amongst the youth especially in Manipur, which was hitherto largely confined to the underground. Above all, it has served as a sort of confirmation of a lingering impression, widely prevalent in the NE, that the Centre does not understand the mindset and sensitivities of the communities of the NE and that if it does, it does not seem to care. That such an appraisal, however biased and unjustified, of the Centre's handling of the NE affairs should still be possible, after over 50 years of our freedom, reflects the unsettled state of affairs in the NE-Centre interaction.

The government claims that the present decision is intended only to widen ceasefire area, without any commitment whatsoever to alter existing State borders. This still begs the question why it took the risk of provoking unrest outside Nagaland at this stage. Why pursue this negotiating strategy? The decision to resume talks at Bangkok must have presumably been based upon the assurance by the Nagas that a peace settlement should be sought within the framework of the Constitution. The two substantial concessions that can be made within this framework are territorial gains and enhanced political autonomy. And territory is one of the cardinal demands of the Naga rebels. If this is not a beginning of territorial concession, then why make the gesture now? Will it not at least partly foreclose the negotiations? The way the government is now trying to explain away its decision appears to be doing just that.

The Language of Pressure

Besides, what cannot, and should not, be taken lightly is the apprehension in the NE that the government might one day "reward" the NSCN simply because the latter is perceived as the most tenacious of the insurgents. A way has also to be found to dispel the notion that the only medium the Centre understands is the language of pressure, lawful or lawless. Any deal to be done at Bangkok will, therefore, have to be mindful of its potential for the domino effect. It should not lose sight of one of its own starting premises that the Naga rebels had been, and still are, an inspiration for a host of insurgent groups in the NE, some of which are strategically viable to become as tenacious as the NSCN. It should remember that "Northeast" is not Kashmir and is not likely ever to be.

It is also important not to draw a parallel with the only `peace accord' the Centre has managed to conclude with an underground group in the NE to date, with that of the Mizo National Front (MNF) of Mizoram in 1986. That was no `peace accord' but an MoU concluded with an increasingly demoralised insurgent outfit, and essentially structured to facilitate `the honourable return' of Laldenga and his men, while at the same time paving the way for the consolidation of the Congress party led by Lal Thanhawla. No reward' of any significance was therefore necessary. The political concessions given to the MNF were hardly more than those already made available for Meghalaya and Arunachal, both of which had not resorted to insurgency.

Alienation of the People

The troubled Northeast does seem to deserve a well thought out and comprehensive plan to tackle its countless problems. If there is such a one, no one has heard of it in the region. Such a plan could go into the underlying reasons behind the `alienation' of the people in general. It could seek ways to combat insurgency at its sources arms supplies, funding, poor management of Indo- Myanmar borders, misinformation, and so on. It could fine-tune and upgrade perhaps the most potent weapon against insurgency economic management of the region, among others, by devising the Centre's system of disbursement of grants and aid less amenable to gross abuse by local politicians. And, above all, it shouid find means to co-opt the innocent and law-abiding majority through various NGOs and voluntary organisations.

9

VISION NER-2020: With Reference to Mizoram

Welcome Remarks

I would like, first of all, to convey our deep appreciation for the gracious presence of our CM as Chief Guest of this Workshop. It was not without some trepidation that we approached him with our request at the last moment. In fact, I dared not do it myself and had to hide behind Pu Denghnuna to do the job.

Indeed, such an endeavour as we are engaged in today can be quite ineffectual if it is not eventually accompanied by a *political will.* That capacity to inject political will into our ongoing exercise resides solely with the Chief Minister. His presence in our midst today is a hopeful sign and a comfort to us.

Let me now welcome Mr. Sanjoy Hazarika, Managing Trustee of C-NES. Most probably, many of you know him personally. He is a man of many important parts. A journalist, writer, film producer, an activist for various good causes in NE and so on, he has always distinguished himself in whatever matters he has set upon himself. In my opinion, he has single-handedly done the most to highlight the varied colored picture of the NE to India's mainstream media. I count myself very lucky to be one of his friends.

Let me now turn to the subject of the Workshop. To put it simply, it is about drawing up a *Wish List* of the people to be incorporated in NER Vision-2020. It must, let me emphasize, never be construed as a criticism of the authorities, past or present. Our endeavor is not just for the NEC; it is also for the Planning Commission, Government of India, the State Government and whoever wishes to make use of it for helping the NE.

In the history of planning, no attempt, as far as I know, has been made to draw up the people's wish list with the express purpose of forming it as the basis of Planning. Our meeting today is therefore unique. In the course of a longish stint I had as an Indian diplomat abroad, I served in 15 countries engaging with various foreign governments. In no country did I see any attempt being made like the one NEC is making this time.

NEC has, indeed, taken a bold risk in throwing this challenge before us. We are here today to meet that challenge. In so doing, we are throwing back another challenge to NEC and the Government of India - a challenge for them to redeem our dreams, our visions. Let us all hope that that will happen in the next 15 years, if not completely, at least substantially.

Center for North-East Studies & Policy Research

Established as a Trust in 2000

6. Mr. Chaman Lal, former DGP, Nagaland
7. Lt. Gen. (Rtd). V. K. Nayar, former Governor of Manipur.

Panel of Advisers:

1. Dr. Jayanti Madhab, Chairman
2. Mr. L.C. Jain, Development Economict
3. Ms. Particia Mukhim, Journalist and Social Activist
4. Mr. N.N. Vohra, IAS (Rtd.)
5. Mr. Denghnuna, IAS (Rtd.)
6. Mr. O.P. Jain, Philanthropist
7. Dr. Suman Sahai, of Gene Campaign
8. Mr. L.T. Pudaite, IFS (Rtd.)

THEME: VISION NER-2020
Indicative Visions

1. Transportation & Information and Communication Technology (ICT):

Transport

Transformation of Northeast India region into a major gateway between South Asia and Southeast Asia / South-west China, in pursuit of India's 'Look East' policy: This will at once eliminate the "isolation and remoteness" of the region and facilitate investment inflows into Northeast, both foreign direct investment (FDI) and domestic, cross border trades, tourism, etc.

Illustrative Recommendations

a. Upgrade, and integrate Mizoram's transport network into existing proposals for Trans-Asian Railways (TAR) and Asian Highway systems; e.g. additional AH linkage from Bangladesh via Agartala - Aizawl -Champhai - Tiddim/Falam -Mandalay.... (The original proposals for TAR and AH systems do not cover Tripura, Mizoram and Chin State of Myanmar!)

b. Connect NH-54 from south Mizoram to Haka in Myanmar.

c. Enhance quality of maintenance of all existing roads to at least all weather level and upgrade load bearing capacity of bridges in all major roads to national standard.

d. Early execution of the Multi-Modal Highway-cum-IWT Project on Kolodyne.

e. Railway (broad-gauge) expansion from Chaparmukh (Assam valley) to Hailakandi (Cachar), bypassing 39 tunnels and 179 bridges in the Lumding to Badarpur sector; then extend railway to Bairabi (Mizoram) upto Lawngtlai/Myanmar border in south Mizoram.

f. To bypass Sonapur area, where the highway frequently blocked by land / mudslides thourhout rainy seasons, another highway link from Assam valley to Surma valley is essential.

g. Open up Inland Water-cum- Rail /Road transit routes from Mizoram to West Bengal via Bangladesh, and also to access Chittagong port.

h. Direct air links en route some Northeast cities to Southeast Asian cities like Kunming, Yangon, Mandalay, Bangkok, etc.

ICT

Mizoram is severely handicapped by the existing 'nominal' and *erratic internet connectivity,* and has thereby been unable to avail of the new *technology-driven opportunities* for advancement that are routinely available to much of the rest of the country. It is not only the absence of reliable speed-communication by which it is disenabled, but it is also 'deprived' of vital data that are essential to keep abreast with the rest of the country in various sectors of development. Thus, essential tools for development planning and implementation such as data banks, various documentations, even project reports models, cannot be accessed and updated in a timely manner. In short, Mizoram is still in the 'branch post office (BPO)' zone in the current 'information revolution' which is being led by India world wide.

Essential Requirement

Provide Mizoram with High Speed Data Communication (HSDC) services with the same connectivity being used by Software Technology Parks of India (STPI) and set up a Sub-Centre at Aizawl, connected to STPI hubs already operating in Guwahati or Kolkata.

2. Energy / Power Generation

Harness at least 10 per cent of estimated 2400 MW of Hydro-power potential in Mizoram, along with sustained promotion of wind and solar energy.

Selected Proposals

a) Execute Tuirial H.E. Project (60 MW), Tuivai H.E. Project (210 MW), Bairabi H.E. Project (80 MW) and Stage I & II Kolodyne Project (MW 500). These together should supply more than 10 p.c. of the estimated power potential in the State even during the period of the leanest water discharge.

b) Encourage NGOs (or even reserve some for them) to engage in mini / micro hydro-power projects and wind / solar power generation in line with GOI's policy of harnessing renewables and non-conventional energy by non-government agencies.

c) To obviate corruption and delay, power generation by renowned firms on a 'turn-key' or 'build - operate - transfer (BOT)' basis may also be encouraged / explored.

d) Include Northeast in projected supply of gas from Rakhine coast (Myanmar) by ONGC and GAIL via pipeline through Mizoram.

e) Handing over of control / management of distribution of domestic consumption of electricity to communities/ local bodies as is done in Nagaland should be explored.

3. Agriculture and Allied Sectors

1) Achieve commercial scale organic farming of selected cash crops such as oil seeds (both edible and bio-fuel), spices, fruits, flowers, crops and herbs rich in nutritional and medicinal values, etc.

2) Attain at least self-reliance and security of supply in locally producible food items such as pork, poultry, fisheries, cattle, dairy and vegetable products.

Such a vision will, among others, involve

a) Encourage **co-operation** to undertake estate farming or compact area farming by small holders in *co-operatives or in Self Help Groups (SHGs).*

b) Construct and maintain link roads to such farming locations and resource rich areas.

c) Rational and fair 'statutory' land use system which should also guarantee *conservation of biodiversity* and adequate *forest* cover.

d) Promote contract farming wherever feasible but with full proof security for farmers.

e) Effective and efficient *Extension Services* in the various sectors including easy access to *Laboratory facilities* should be made available by the State government.

f) Identification and selection of crops and suitable areas for their *organic* cultivation on a scientific basis, particularly of those that can be *processed (finished/semi-finished)* before they are marketed outside the State except, perhaps, in the case of flowers.

4. Governance

Decentralization of governance accompanied by adequate financial power vested with local authorities at all levels. Autonomous administrative bodies for urban centers, districts, blocks and villages should be created, perhaps, along similar lines to the Panchayti Raj system enacted by the Parliament. This requires legislation.

5. Gender Issues

Essentially pertinent also to governance is participation of women in it. No governance can be truly democratic without the participation of 'half' of the population. And their participation cannot be ensured by opinion poll alone. There should, therefore, be a *statutory guarantee* for a reasonable level of women's participation in all elected organs of governance. This will help ensure removal of injustices to women.

6. Social Sectors (Education and Health Care)

A 'Vision' for 2020 in education should be ideally prepared by an impartial, expert and experienced non-governmental Commission charged with an open-ended terms of reference. It can be constituted by NGOs with mass membership such as YMA, MHIP, MUP, Churches, etc., which should on their part ensure the mandatory adherence to the recommendations of the Commission by any future ministries. The Commission could, beside others, examine:

a) The feasibility or otherwise of 'communitization' of pre-primary and primary education as has been experimented in Nagaland;

b) The role of private, 'commercial' schools: how to regulate their mushrooming, to stop it or to enter into partnership with them. Above all, a way has to be found to ensure the implementation of the policy of 'universal education' for all children without the parents having to pay exorbitant fees to private operators.

In the *Health care* sector, the management of primary health and care Centres should perhaps be handed over to the communities as is being done in Nagaland and Arunachal. A way has to be found by which every family has an access to *health insurance*. This is a minimum need in the context of the problems of instituting comprehensive 'social security system' in India at the present stage. Government - Private partnership for complementary services in health care can also be strengthened. While supply of safe drinking water is the responsibility of the authorities, the management of fair distribution of water and effective control of its quality is better managed by local communities.

7. People's Participation in Planning and Project Implementation

The power that be and concerned officials have seemed to be wary of the participation of the stake holders / beneficiaries in the processes of planning and implementation of projects. Nor are they inclined to be transparent in their operations. Despite the passage of the 'Right to Information Act, 2005' the implementing authorities will still need to be induced to enlist effective public participation. Full public participation can be ensured only by the custodians of the keys to 'funding and sanctions', namely, NEC, DONER and the Planning Commission.

Apart from insisting on strict adherence to the Non-Lapsable Central Pool of Resources for the Northeast (NLCPR) Guidelines, these three agencies should make it mandatory:

a) To keep the public - intended stake holders / beneficiaries – informed fully of any projects concerned with them at the planning stage.

b) To ensure public participation in monitoring and evaluation of the execution of such projects, it should be mandatory for a group of non-official stake holders to be set up to perform the tasks.

c) To ensure and facilitate if necessary designation or formation of an NGO / NGOs for the above purposes.

Summary of Responses to Questionnaire

1. Respondents - Sex-wise:	Male - 60 %
2. Average Age:	35 - 55 years
3. Marital Status:	Married - 80%
4. Educational Status:	Secondary - 65%, Above - 35%
5. Family:	Joint - 85%, Nuclear - 15%
6. Residence / House	Own - 95%, Rented - 5%
7. Average Family Size:	6 Members

8. Migration: Residents of Aizawl, Serchhip, Champhai, Kolasib, Mamit and Lunglei Districts have all been migrants at one time or another due to 'regrouping of villages' during the disturbances. Lawngtlai, Saiha and Chawngte District residents are mostly permanent except some Chakma migrants from Bangladesh who do not indicate their status at all.

9. Occupation: Agriculture - 62%, Self-employed - 35%,

Govt. - Rest

I. Change or Not:	No - 55%, Yes - 45%
II. Satisfactory / No:	No - 65%, Yes - 35%
III. Adequate Income / No:	N0 - 78%, Yes - 22%

10. Insignificant Response - most of them rear pigs...

11. I. School going children:	99.6%.
II. Govt. / Private:	Govt. - 67%, Private - 33%
IV. Drop Out:	57 cases out of 3000
V. Reason:	Blame on child's negligence
VI. Quality of Education:	Poor - 67%, 33 - no choice

12. Gender Issues:

I. Women participation:	Yes, in their own social groups

II. In Favour:	About 100%
III. Women SHHG:	Yes, about minus-half
IV. Grant/Contract to SHHG:	Majority
V. Violence to Women:	About 30 %

13. Development Schemes: Nobody has been Consulted
14. Health: common disease - malaria, skin disease, jaundice, dysentery and cost of treatment: not affordable, Water supply, poor; immunization done universally.
15. Nutrition: Good with little meat.
16. Communication: Misunderstood, mostly due to unawareness.
17. Governance: Not Satisfied, mostly.

10

COMMENTS AND SUGGESTIONS*

Introduction

The primary impediment to the development process in the Northeast (NE) region has continued to be the absence or lack of effective involvement of the grassroots level / stake holders in the process of planning, and in the monitoring and evaluation of the execution of development programs. This has remained the main corruption enabling factor, often resulting in tardy or shoddy and, even in failure of, implementation of projects. Therefore, the *strategy aimed at ensuring participation of the civil society* in the monitoring and evaluation of the execution of development programs need to be strengthened. Participation by the stake holders could, perhaps, be made conditional for funding of projects, and an inbuilt mechanism to ensure such participation could be incorporated in the sanctioning process.

Grassroots participation in the detailed planning processes may not be always feasible, but a mechanism can be devised to monitor their felt needs and aspirations. Last year, for example, the North Eastern Council (NEC) initiated the formulation of what it termed **'VISION NER -2020'** by means of direct consultations with large sections of the population in the entire NE region. The task of monitoring public opinion was outsourced to the *Centre for North East*

---

* Submitted to the Steering Committee of Planning Commission on 'Empowerment of Scheduled Tribes

Studies & Policy Research (C-NES), New Delhi, which in turn entrusted the work of ground level survey to selected NGOs operating in the respective NE States. (The Tribal Welfare Agency, our NGO, was given the responsibility for Mizoram). Actual 'Vision' survey was done by means of Questionnaires (and Indicative Visions in the case of Mizoram), responses to which were personally verified and collected by Enumerators from carefully selected families and community organizations in the various RD Blocks. A series of workshops and seminars were also held, involving knowledgeable members of civil society and officials. The outcome of the survey appeared to reflect fairly accurately the opinions of the populace at large. As a large number of the respondents are members of the Scheduled Tribes, the Reports of NEC could, perhaps, be used by the Planning Commission as sample inputs in its current exercise. (Copies of the Questionnaire and Indicative Visions for Mizoram are enclosed).

Topical Points of Interest for NE

Following are some points of vital relevance to the development of NE region, and are listed not necessarily in order of priority:

Transparency in Development Programs

Stake holders / beneficiaries should be associated with the initiation of project ideas so that they are aware of what to expect right from the start. This will also help them to effectively involve in the preparation and the execution process of the projects.

Attempts to bring about transparency through monitoring committees often do not work as long as the authority to appoint such committees is vested solely with the ruling party/government or the officials of the department concerned. Checks and balances should be put in place not just in the operation of the monitoring body but right at the time of constituting such bodies. Members of opposition parties as well as impartial NGOs / leading members of civil society, on equal footing with the officials concerned, should jointly initiate the forming of monitoring bodies. The person who heads such bodies should be preferably non-official and, if need be, entitled to appropriate honorarium.

Shifting Cultivation

Most of the farming communities in the hills region of NE continue to practice shifting cultivation for lack of viable alternatives. With a steady depletion and reduced fertility of *jhum* lands, these communities are increasingly powerless and vulnerable to exploitation by the newly emerging political and business elites. Even after fifty years of independence, the efforts of the State governments to provide them with alternative income generating occupations have so far made no significant headway.

Take the case of Mizoram for example. The state governments took up 'Garden Colonies' in the early 80s, then New Land Use Policy (NLUP) in the late 80s and 90s and since 2002 what is termed as Mizoram Intodelh Project (MIP) or Mizoram Self-reliance Project. Under these schemes, farmers are given assistance in cash, which the impoverished marginal farmer is often not able to plough into producing whatever crops he has chosen in a settled farm / plantation, resulting in a failure of the scheme. At the end of the day, these farmers often have no choice but to sell the plots of land allotted to them to wealthy urbanites, thereby unwittingly giving rise to a (absentee) landed gentry and depleting even more cultivable farmlands available to rural farmers. In short, for these and other complex reasons such as political partisanship and favoritism on the part of the authorities concerned, the schemes to provide alternatives to *jhum* cultivators have often been flawed right from the stage of selection process of the farmer- beneficiaries. Much development monies have thus been wasted by the State governments in the name of such schemes.

To wean away, as it were, mostly uneducated farmers from their age-old habit and practice of shifting cultivation obviously requires well thought out plan. Just handing out small amounts of cash to them without sustained support in terms of extension and other needed services would not do. It should perhaps be seen as a long term investment in human and physical capitals, with direct connection to conservation of forests, biodiversity and the environment. The problem could be more comprehensively conceived as one covering the settlement problems of nomadic tribal communities in the fringes of forests. As such, it does seem to deserve a serious Central intervention, either in the form of Central Boards or Agencies promoting specific missions and operating at least for a period of five years or more.

An *Alternative Suggestion* is that the entire mission to wean farmers away from the practice of shifting cultivation may be brought under the programs of *Centrally Sponsored Schemes*, to be implemented by NGOs under the guidance and monitoring of technologically competent agencies. Much of the hill areas of NE have been identified, for instance, by the Spices Board as suitable for farming selected spices like turmeric, black pepper, large cardamom, etc. Under the centrally sponsored Horticulture Technology Mission, selected flowers such as bird of paradise and anthurium have been successfully promoted. Oil bearing seeds like red palm oil and jatropha are also found to be thriving in these areas. In other words, only those crops which have been experimentally proven to be suitable for local conditions may be taken up under this scheme.

The existing efforts of the Spices Board and the Horticulture Mission can also be brought under this scheme, with additional funding from the Centre. Such an arrangement will be able to tie up several loose ends that had stood in the way of successful implementation of the schemes:

1. Projects will be made only under the guidance of experts in the field and in consultation with the beneficiaries, who are responsible to implement them.
2. Funding will be made available only after the viability of the project is vetted from all angles.
3. Implementation will be under guidance of technically competent personnel such as from Spices Board or State Government or as stipulated by the Centre.
4. Projects can be taken up in phases under controlled conditions by the sanctioning authority.
5. There will be no scope for meddling by vested interests of officials or politicians.

Bringing such relevant schemes as has been distributed under the Spices Board, NOVOD, Silk Board, Horticulture Mission, Coffee and Tea Boards, etc. together and placing these under one nodal authority at the State level for implementation in collaboration with NGOs can also be considered. Micro-credit and rainwater harvesting schemes will also be required as follow up support for the program.

Control / Supervision of NGOs

Many department officials of State Governments have set up NGOs consisting of their spouses or relatives "to make use" of CSS funding available under their respective fields of activities. This is contrary to the spirit of voluntary efforts for development. Forming of such NGOs by persons connected with officials should be banned and the existing ones should be disbanded. At any rate, a Central Bureau for screening and accrediting NGOs should be set up.

Empowerment of Local Bodies

No adequately empowered local bodies have been instituted in some of the NE States, as intended by the constitutional Amendments 73 and 74. For example, Mizoram's

Village Councils have no authorities and power that can be remotely compared to those of Panchayats in other States. As the result, finances earmarked for them continue to be controlled by the Local Administration Department (LAD) at the state level. Application of the Panchayats (Extension to the Scheduled Areas) Act, 1996, or similar arrangements, to these States could be considered. Unless this anomaly is rectified, the idea of empowerment of local bodies remains meaningless to the rural poor in these States.

The reason for the State level authorities' reluctance to concede power to control finances to local bodies is obvious. The Centre could consider withholding release of funds designated by the Finance Commission for use by local bodies, until and unless GOI is satisfied that proper local authorities have been put in place by these NE states. Even if PESA Act, 1996 cannot be suitably extended to NE for some reasons, there is need to gently 'compel' these States to cede their financial powers to properly constituted local authorities. Only then, real rural development, including alternatives to shifting cultivation and stake-holder participation, could take place.

Primary Health & Education

A system could be evolved whereby control and management of primary education and health could be handed over to the communities concerned, while funding should continue to be provided by the government. This experiment has been tried successfully in Arunachal and Nagaland under what is termed as *Communitization*. Unless a system to guarantee at least a minimum of *health insurance* is evolved for the rural poor, much of the health facilities will remain inaccessible to them. This appears to be a much needed essential measure to complement the *Rural Employment Guarantee* scheme.

ICT

The physical isolation and remoteness of NE can be

sharply reduced by enabling the NE to make use of the advances of IT, especially internet enabled services. A special Task Force group to develop such facilities in NE ought to be set up. Well before physical connectivity is brought to the place under India's Look East policy, NE could have been connected, while generating much needed jobs among the educated unemployed. A special IT training school or scholarships could be instituted for the steadily increasing number of educated unemployed in NE.

Managing Director,
Tribal Welfare Agency,
Aizawl, Mizoram.

11

THE BASIC PRINCIPLES OF INDIAN FOREIGN POLICY

The 'foreign policy' of India is not nearly foreign from its domestic priorities, as the term may seem to suggest. It is, indeed, fundamentally intended to safeguard our vital national interests abroad and can even be regarded as the extension of our domestic policies. India's essential interests - for the sake of convenient description - can be broadly articulated under three headings:

One - consolidation and preservation of our national independence;

Two - safeguarding of our national security; and

Three - national development in its most comprehensive sense.

Underlying our approach to these primary and pragmatic concerns and the method by which we have attempted to tackle them, are the *values and ideals* we inherited from our past, such as the spirit of tolerance and cooperation, non-violence, truthfulness, and the pursuit of democratic and secular values. We also seek to project and promote these *ideals,* wherever feasible, in the course of our interaction with other countries.

We shall now briefly describe how the aforementioned ideas are translated into aspects of our foreign policy and how they are executed in the process of the actual conduct of the foreign affairs of India. Due to the limited time allotted to this talk, our explanations will have to be brief and only illustrative.

Independence - In order to consolidate, maintain and strengthen our independence from the British rule in 1947, the first and foremost need for us was to be free of any dominating influence from any quarters. The only options open to us then were - to be tied in alliance with either of the opposing camps of the *cold war,* (the communist bloc led by the Soviet Union and the capitalist group spearheaded by the USA), *or* to remain unaligned and position ourselves at an equidistance from these two adversarial blocks. We chose to remain independent and adopted what is now famously known as the *policy of non-alignment.* Non-alignment is not passive neutrality but an active involvement in all-major international issues in accordance with our own lights and perspectives, and independent judgment.

Our adherence to the policy of non-alignment was manifested most clearly in our actions in the course of our participation in the deliberations of the United Nation, for examples, on questions such as the Middle East, Indo-China, colonialism, major economic issues confronting the developed and developing countries, etc. On all these and subsequent issues, we sought to inject what might be termed as the non-aligned sense of fairness and justice; and for this reason, we were often misunderstood and disliked by both the opposing blocs of the cold war. Our distaste for alliance system was demonstrated early by our refusal to join the South-East Asian Treaty Organisation (SEATO) and the Baghdad Pact. Over time, however, particularly after the easing of cold war tensions, our independent policy has been amply vindicated.

National Security - To safeguard our national security from external threat as well as from internal turmoil, and to maintain our national integrity, we needed to achieve an adequate strength and self-reliance, both military and economic. To maintain even a minimum military strength or a credible deterrent defensive force - enough to ensure our national security - is an enormous drain on our national resources and an impediment to our development plans. Besides, the idea of fortifying ourselves by sheer military might is not in keeping without national ethos of tolerance and non-violence. Hence, our founding fathers foresaw the futility of military force per se, and decided to pursue the path of *peaceful co-existence among nations* as a durable guarantee for national security. India was thus one of the founding signatories of the *Bandung* declaration on the Five Principles of Peaceful Co-existence among Nations or the *Panchsheel* as it has come to be known.

The Five Principles of Peaceful Co-existence were first formulated in the preamble to the agreement between India and China in regard to Tibet in April, 1954 and were unanimously adopted, in a slightly different wording, by a UN resolution in 1957. The principles are: 1. Mutual respect for each other's territorial integrity and sovereignty; 2. Mutual non-aggression; 3. Mutual non-interference in each other's internal affairs; 4. Equality and mutual benefit; and 5. Peaceful co-existence. We have always endeavored to apply these principles in our interaction with other countries. With our immediate neighbours, including China and Pakistan, we have sought to enhance the quality of our cooperation - by advocating the policy of *good neighbourliness.*

Development - When we speak of development in the present context, it is in its most pervasive sense - which includes all the segments of cultural, political and socio-economic progress that are essential for building a dynamic nation state. There can be no meaningful development in conditions of confrontation and war. The essential requisite for us to be able to focus on the work of development is a peaceful and tension-free environment in our neighbourhood and regions beyond. We therefore advocated and insisted that *friendly relations with our immediate neighbours,* such as Bangladesh, Nepal, Sri Lanka and, particularly, with Pakistan, are necessary conditions for development in our region. Along with them, we created the South Asian Association for Regional Cooperation (SAARC); and, with this instrument and by various other means at our disposal, we have largely been able to increase our cooperative interactions with our neighbours, including even with Pakistan, despite lingering problems which do not lend themselves to simple solutions such as border and other historical disputes.

While peace is an essential condition for development, there can be no lasting peace where countries vie for military superiority to their neighbours or others. There is bound to be tension in an environment of arms race. An enduring peace, indeed durable world peace, can only be achieved if the world is free of competition in the building of weaponry. We recognize that *disarmament* is the ultimate requirement for global peace and development. We have therefore been one of the most active and engaged participants in the UN Conference on disarmament, held from time to time in Geneva. India's proposal for credible and predictable *programme for comprehensive disarmament* (including complete destruction of nuclear weapons) has remained today one of the major UN documents, pending for detailed negotiations.

Ideals - As a country richly endowed with diverse religions, languages, even cultures and races, we have come to learn to value the democratic ideals we inherited from the past. Without mutual tolerance and accommodation, in a non-violent and secular environment, and a strong desire for peaceful co-existence - indeed, without these essential ingredients of democracy, we might not have been even able to survive as a united and vibrant country. Just as we realize the value of these ideals for our own existence and welfare, we sought to apply them in our dealings with other countries. Right from the early years of our independent existence as a nation, we advocated *peaceful negotiations* for the resolution of disputes, peaceful *dialogues,* instead of confrontation, for countries or groups of them with differing view points.

Even in the hey days of the struggles against colonial domination, in which we were in the forefront, true to our own mode of struggle, we encourages non-violent modes and tried to discourage violent means. In short, in all international interactions, whether it is between a powerful nation and a weak one, between a rich and a poor country, or a socialist and a capitalist one, we have always promoted a *peaceful mode of dialogue between nations.*

12

UNION CHRISTIAN COLLEGE (U.C.C.) MY LITTLE OXFORD

The depth of my indebtedness to the U.C.C. cannot be fathomed without some understanding of my educational and general background prior to my joining the college. I came from a village, which was located at a good three days' walk from the nearest motorable dirt road. Our family's economic status could be categorized as lower middle class in the then rather impoverished rural Mizoram. The teacher of the elementary school, where I undertook my first formal study, was class VII fail, while the headmaster of the middle school I went to was just class VIII pass. At high school too, I did full year terms for only classes VII and X. As my mother passed away while I was studying in class VII, I had to help my father in farming; I could not go to school for classes VIII and IX and had to appear for promotion examination as a private candidate. Thus, when I joined the college, even though, I had not had an adequate academic experience and knowledge usually necessary for transition to university education.

I joined the U.C.C. in September 1958, about a month after the classes begun. The day I arrived at Barapani, it was raining heavily. I had to walk from G.S. road, which was at the bottom of the present Barapani dam, carrying my tin suitcase and a quilt in a hold-all. Halfway to the college, I met Prof. Hamlet Bareh, who was then, if I recall correctly, teaching Khasi. Upon seeing me completely drenched to the skin, he offered to help me carry my baggage. We hinged the straps of my hold-all to the stem of his umbrella and jointly carried it, much like the butchers do to their merchandise while transporting it on foot! As a consequence, poor Prof. Bareh, his well-pressed suit got completely soaked in the rain !

On arrival at the campus, Prof. Bareh took me straight to acting Principal Simon's house, where I was dried and fed with a delicious Khasi dinner. I was then taken to the evening church service, at the end of which I was asked to introduce myself, enabling me to have a glimpse for the first time of what seemed then formidably sophisticated faces of my college-mates-to be. I was then led to the 'room' allotted to me, a corner of the basement hall of the 'High Hall' (I hope the name hasn't been changed). Finally, there arrived my first night at a college, as far as I was concerned, an ambition, an impossible dream come true!

Life in college had painful teething problems; in my case, mainly for lack of money and for the lingering hope that I had had of pursuing theological studies rather than secular education. As I could not buy all the needed text books initially, for the first few months I relied heavily on the lecture notes I took by means of my own shorthand device. I remember how I used to struggle to record Fr. Kuriakose's lectures on Logic, delivered in chaste Malayali English at a very high frequency.

I had many memorable experiences at the U.C.C. To record all of them will take a book. Owing to lack of self-confidence and to social uncertainty, for months I was withdrawn and did not mix much. I was not even confident that I would make the grade in the first term exam. I did make intensive use of the library though, throughout my tenure. According to the then Librarian, I borrowed more books at any given time than anyone else but Mrs. Taylor, wife of the next Principal.

Apart from the surprise at passing the first term exam, what really drew me out of my self-imposed cocoon was a debate competition. I can't quite figure out now what persuaded me to participate in it. Prepare for it, I did very seriously. I would climb alone the hills above the hostel and make my speech on a mound, pretending it was a podium. I would slam my tongue with a pencil between my teeth while trying to pronounce difficult English sounds. The methodical practice won me the first prize to my utter surprise. By now everyone realized that I wasn't that shy or introvert, just a bit quiet on my private ambitions. Then, it was time to melt with the crowd.

Many hilarious evenings were provided to us by the odd practice of setting up camp fire after the dinner. It was started by Bah Ngur (Ngurchhona). In those days, in dry seasons, there were plenty of dry reeds and tree barks to burn just next to the Windham Hall. We would sit around the fire and recite poems, tell stories or folklores, or simply lapse into crude jokes and some vulgarities or another. The regular partakers of this club were G. Edwin Warson, David Bathew, Martin Khongmen, Ngurchhona, Bah Arnold, Chonglienthang Changsan and Vanh L. Hruaia. many "associate" members were also there. Little did we realize then, what a Freudian release our indulgence might have provided us.

As for the academic assets I acquired from the U.C.C. there is little point in trying to explain them in detail. As already made obvious at the outset, my dependence for education on the U.C.C was so total that to describe its process will mean explaining each new stage of learning. The memories of the excitement and delight at the discovery of new knowledge and the feelings of frustration, at times, at the slow pace of my comprehension have, however remained fresh with me today. I recall, for example, how my head reeled when I read for the first time Mahatma

Gandhi's "*My Experiments with Truth*" and got completely convinced of the validity of his approach. Alas, due to my youthful lack of sense of balance, it had to be at the expense of my erstwhile admiration for Jawaharlal Nehru ! In short, U.C.C. is what Oxford, Sorbonne or Harvard is to many of my international colleagues.

The influences I felt from some of the teachers are perhaps apt here. Whatever understanding of the English language I have today, I owe it almost entirely to Prof. Ivan Simon, who was then acting as Principal. He made me read "King's English" seven times over and I used to submit to him weekly extra essays, which he would correct in red ink. I can still feel the pang of frustration when I saw his correction of my first paper, which was splashed with red ink all over. Prof. Brian Minty of Oxford was another teacher whom I could regard as a friend. Even though I could never emulate it, my familiarity with his impeccable Oxonian accent was to help me much, later in life. His humility, his dedication to service and openness of mind also provided a lasting example.

My encounter with the present principal, Dr. C.J. John, is also still vivid. He was my psychology and comparative religions teacher in philosophy (Hons.) class, which he often conducted in his own house. I was deeply impressed by his capacity to organize his time and affairs, and his detachment from humdrum pettiness. For my lack of enthusiasm for ancient religions, I hope, I made it up by my mild addiction to sports and physical exercise, which was largely inspired by him and was to help me remain fit even today.

The man who stood above all others among my early influences was Principal Dr. H. John Taylor. I stood up to him on many occasions with a different opinion. He was always fair and objective in the manner of his consideration of others' views. As he himself was not only an outstanding educationist but also an eminent nuclear physicist, to feel that one could engage him on a one-man to one-man basis was to gain in intellectual confidence.

While suggesting this article to me, Principal John also wanted me to include in it my 'vision for the U.C.C'. However, I must not pretend that for all these years I have remained that involved with the U.C.C. that I actually have a specific vision for it. The best I can do would perhaps be to give a sort of a brief message. Life itself is an opportunity to better ourselves. The information we gather and the skill we acquire, and indeed science and technology should serve to enrich the inner springs of life, to quicken our sense of value and our sense of responsibility to the family of humankind, to our very survival and even to the survival of our planet.

Yet, as we prepare to enter the 21st century, the overwhelming number of us appears to be only obscurely aware of the decline we cause to the human spirit by our pursuit of simple greed and shortsighted selfishness. To redeem our civilization, we need a recovery of spiritual awareness and a halt to our wanton assault on nature in the name of development. It is my earnest hope and prayer that the U.C.C may send forth in many years to come men and women of vision and courage, of wisdom and virtue, who are incapable of fear and intolerant of injustice.

13

IDENTITY

I am grateful to Paul B. Chonzik for introducing me to the hmaryahoogroup. These last few weeks, I have been browsing occasionally your postings. To say it simply, I have been delighted with the opinions and the information with which you have often surprised me.

As a member of the group, I thought it is about time I should also contribute some comments. After all, I considered, a membership of any group entails participation, however meagre that may be. For the present, I shall confine myself to what seems to me the main preoccupation of the Group:

1. Identity

I have never been confused about my identity. I was born in Khawlek village in Mizoram, to a Leiri family belonging to Hmar tribe. My mother was of the Lungtau clan (Nungate) while my father belonged to the Pudaite family of the Leiri clan. My mother spoke to my father in Lusei while my father spoke to her in Hmar dialect. We the children also spoke to our mother in Lusei dialect, at the same time speaking to our father in Hmar language. We were bilingual everyday of our lives. I was the eldest of four children. My youngest sister, who was born in 1946, begun to use only Lusei to communicate with us. This was obviously because more and more people were speaking in Lusei and that dialect begun to be regarded as the lingua franca in our village. This was about early 1950s. I told my sister that as far as we were concerned, we were to communicate only in our own mother tongue, which is Hmar. That has continued till today.

In those days, all the residents of 'Lushai Hills' were technically Lushais. Since we were factually and historically not Lushais (which was an obvious reference to Luseis), I used to shudder at the thought that I might one day be required to identify myself formally in writing on record. I was clear that I was not a Lusei, but a Hmar, at the same time, that I was akin to those who call themselves 'Lushais'. There were also a sizable group of Paites in our village, who were like us very keen on preserving their identity and different dialect. Then I went off to Senvon to join class 5 in a Middle English School in 1949. I found to my surprise that the Hmar population was enthusiastically taking part in the Mizo Union movement. As I was little, I didn't really know what it amounted to. But I surmised that the 'Mizo thing' was the solution to my feeling of separateness from the 'Lushais.' Now, I thought, we could belong to an identity larger than our respective tribes and all feel belong to it. In fact, I used to report eagerly to my father, who was then the Treasurer of the Mizo Union Unit in our village about the activities of the Mizo Union movement. Then, it became very clear to me that Mizo is composed of many tribes such as Hmar, Lusei, Ralte, Thado, Paite, etc. and those that may yet to be identified. That was when my heart and mind rested, dissolving the anxiety about my identity.

Since then, whenever I had the chance, I was telling others that this was the happy discovery and the historical trend. In College, I used to draw a map of Mizo occupied territory, 'Greater Mizoram'. I was perhaps more than the 'MNF types' in my longing for an abode for our 'nation'. But then this was sentimental. Even then I was certain that a rebellion of the kind MNF launched was impractical and foredoomed.

Index

Index

***